Contents

Foreword

I came to know Mamtimin Ala when he arrived at the Institute of Philosophy, KU Leuven, Belgium to undertake a BA in philosophy. He completed that very well, even though initially his time was accompanied by the cultural shock of living in a foreign country and culture, and even though in the background the descent into tyrannous colonization proceeded apace in his native home, East Turkistan. He continued his studies at the MA level and completed them at the PhD level, again under circumstances that could not be described as easy. I supervised his MA thesis as well as his PhD, hence I got to know him well as his teacher. Mamtimin Ala acquitted himself very well in his studies, though again, despite the silence and calm of study, monstrous things were taking shape at home that touched him to the core. In all of this, and against the backdrop of a kind of anguish, his intelligence, genuineness as a human being, and his considered thoughtfulness were always in evidence.

I speak as one who knows of the situation in East Turkistan from reports in the press and, more importantly, from the witness of Mamtimin Ala himself. Since his time of arrival in Belgium the situation in his home deteriorated further and further. As a witness he could not remain silent, and this made it impossible for him to return to his homeland. Eventually he sought and was granted political asylum in Australia. Since then his torment in relation to what is happening in his home, as well as the urgency of his witness to it, has not ceased. This book is a continuation of this witness. The voice of this singular witness is now lucid and forthright in this indispensable book.

In recent years, forebodings concerning the dimensions of what is occurring in East Turkistan have grown in report after report that have appeared, forebodings that are re-doubled by the appearance of "normality" that the authorities have tried to communicate as the real situation there. This makes this book all the more indispensable in helping the world come to appreciate something of the horrifying ordeal of the Uyghur people that is taking place. I myself do not have direct knowledge of what is occurring. Mamtimin himself acknowledges that now he himself is cut off from his homeland, making his witness all the more complex and difficult. He lays all this out in this important book. When speaking of a witness the most important consideration is the trustworthiness of the one who witnesses. I am willing to vouch for this witness.

I have known Mamtimin for a good number of years as his teacher. We have had many hours of conversations about ethics in relation to others, in relation to the enigmas of human identity, and the perplexities involved in communication, to name just some of the things we discussed. My conversation with him, my meeting with him, left the indelible impression of an entirely genuine human being, a person of intellectual and ethical integrity whose words were to be taken with great seriousness. It is this indelible impression of the unimpeachable trustworthiness of this witness that impels me to recommend this book, and indeed to recommend it urgently. Mamtimin should not only be read and heard but something of the urgency of ultimacy should be heard from his words. These words are born in the torture of the exile, a torture suffered in the remove of the exile who is trying to keep in mind the torture of his own people. This book is an attempt to communicate this mindfulness and share it with those who would hear of the evil visited on his people.

When evil is at work in the dimensions here portrayed one is brought to a pause, and the experience is one of being at a loss as to how to respond to it. There is something almost too much about the thought of this evil, and one is made unsure how to respond. And yet respond we must. Mamtimin has responded in this book, as well as in other ways. For all the reasons above suggested, this is a book that one recommends whole-heartedly, for its trustworthy witness—even though the heart is made heavy with dismay, and sorrow and indignation at the almost unbelievable injustice done to his people.

William Desmond
David Cook Chair in Philosophy, Villanova University, USA
Thomas A. F. Kelly Visiting Chair in Philosophy,
Maynooth University, Ireland
Professor of Philosophy Emeritus, Institute of Philosophy,
KU Leuven, Belgium

Chapter One

Why Do I Write this Book?

I am a Uyghur. As you read this book, you will learn what that statement fully means.

To begin with, I must tell you what this book is not. This book is not an academic thesis analyzing the current situation of Uyghurs in East Turkistan (referred to by Chinese authorities as Xinjiang Uyghur Autonomous Region to hide its colonial past). Nor is this a piece of investigative journalism, intended to describe what is happening. Finally, it is not an anthropological or sociological treatise, supported by field research in the Uyghur native homeland. So, what type of book is this? This book is a reflection from several different angles on the horrific and abhorrent ordeal that Uyghurs are going through in the twenty-first century, as they desperately struggle for survival.

In this book, I aim to discuss the three topics: Why are Uyghurs going through the darkest and most destructive time in their history, a genocide perpetrated by the Chinese Communist Party (CCP)? How is this ordeal affecting them? How is the world reacting to their plight? I examine these questions within a certain context. This Uyghur nightmare is taking place in China, which is paradoxically propagating its image as a benevolent country, making a great contribution to the economic prosperity of the world through the "Chinese Dream"(中国梦). And at the heart of this reflection lies the age-old question that has ever perplexed humanity: What is evil?

I have filtered my reflections through the lenses of philosophical, psychological, and political perspectives. They are unified in such a way that they encompass the fundamental discontentment of Uyghur existence in the past, present, and future. The Uyghur crisis is, by nature, a form of cultural genocide. This assault is politically motivated, resulting in a slow but sure destruction of the psyche of Uyghurs, who are losing their cultural and religious

1

identity both at home and in exile. These three perspectives, therefore, form the foundation for my reflections and will serve as a methodological framework for the narrative of this book.

I will confess that it is not easy to reflect on this crisis, not because of its enormity beyond imagination, but because of my ambiguous relationship to it. I am a Uyghur in exile, so like millions of other Uyghurs, I am a victim of this very genocide—albeit indirectly. But as a person who enjoys reflecting on the human condition in general, I feel driven to write not only about the unbearable pain of Uyghurs as my people, but also about one of the worst human rights catastrophes of the twenty-first century. This is a story told in the context of humanity, highlighting universal implications for human rights and global enlightenment ideals and the current failure to deliver on promises of progress. It illuminates a consistent failure to move towards the emancipation of humanity in an area where there still exists widespread suppression and injustice.

Ultimately, I am questioning the conscience of humanity, which currently prefers silence to action while Uyghurs are too incapacitated by the CCP to defend themselves. I see it as both a personal and universal responsibility to write about this crisis, revealing the troubled relationship between totalitarianism and universal justice, individual rights and state dictatorship, religious prejudices and persecution. I intend to examine the Uyghur crisis by discussing the discontentment due to the lack of universal justice we are facing, while simultaneously analyzing universal justice through the discontentment caused by the Uyghur crisis.

My second role is different from the first one—I am also a storyteller. The story I am telling and reflecting on is a unique one. It is the story of the millions of Uyghurs inside and outside of the concentration camps in East Turkistan who, due to suppression by the CCP, are unable to tell it themselves. Many are in captivity *en masse* and are forbidden to tell their stories or, more disturbingly, they may have died before they were able to share them, which is in itself a story to be told. Uyghurs who are now in exile face threats against any family members and friends who are still captive in our motherland, under the merciless hands of the CCP. Within this context, telling this story is a heavy burden I choose to bear, knowing that my mother, father, siblings, and friends (if they are still alive) may be further persecuted by the CCP as a result of my efforts.

Uyghurs need somebody to tell their forgotten, forbidden, and abhorrent story to the world, and I am this storyteller—a self-appointed advocate for them. Uyghurs inside the camps do not know me as a person or a storyteller, nor do they know what I am going to write about and for them. Even I, to be perfectly honest, am not sure where to start and where to end their story. So why, then, should I write their story?

First, I am an intrinsic part of this story. I am both a victim and a bystander, a strange position to occupy as a storyteller. On the other hand, I acknowledge that as a storyteller, I must be professional, objective, and fair. Objectivity is a challenge, as I am expected to distance myself from the story in which I am ineluctably implicated and emotionally entangled. Consequently, I aim to be emotionally detached, unsympathetically balanced, and ethically impartial. However, this does not mean that I must be apathetic to the suffering of my own people, let alone my own suffering, in order to tell this story professionally. In this writing, I cannot ignore my own cultural identity, being one and the same as that of my people who are being persecuted, their culture destroyed.

My greatest challenge is to look at my own suffering from someone else's perspective, one that provides me with the opportunity to understand my suffering at a deeper level, to externalize and examine it through a proper conceptual framework. It requires me to be impartial while delving into the intrigues and ambiguities of the Uyghur crisis, without relinquishing my right to be ethically relevant, to be ethically non-apathetic, to the stories that I am telling.

To write about this tragedy is an immense challenge, an attempt to speak about the unspeakable. The history of the Holocaust has revealed to us how difficult it is to perceive and think about genocide rationally. It is a concept that exceeds the boundaries of rationality, the limits of thought, language and representation. The greatest challenge in rendering the depth of pain and suffering of the Holocaust is finding a way to rationalize something that lies beyond any rational concepts, to speak of the unspeakable and conceive of the inconceivable cruelty, torture and trauma. "Auschwitz negates all systems, destroys all doctrines. They cannot but impoverish the experience which lies beyond our reach. Ask any survivor and he will tell you, and his children will tell you. [. . .] Between our memory and its reflection there stands a wall that cannot be pierced. The past belongs to the dead and the survivor does not recognize himself in the words linking him to them. We speak in code, we survivors, and this code cannot be broken, cannot be deciphered, not by you no matter how much you try" says Elie Wiesel.[1] Attempting to represent the un-representable, writing shows its innate limitations—its poverty, destitution, and despair.

How do I, then, discuss the Uyghur genocide and do it justice? How do I acknowledge the loss of each soul, silenced or lost forever in a massive network of concentration camps? How will I remain faithful to the same story of those whose perceptions of it have been conversely controlled and altered, and whose thoughts have been re-engineered to accept the humiliation and cruelty, and to think prescriptively, saying only what they are allowed to say? They may even assert that I have fabricated this story about their suffering, and deny it ever actually happened, as is often the case for those experiencing post-traumatic stress disorder. Perhaps they will say I am the one who is brainwashed, that I am vilifying the benign intention of the CCP aiming only to improve Uyghurs' lives by freeing their minds from "risky" and "self-destructive" thoughts. It is difficult speaking on behalf of those who have the right to speak, think, and rationalize freely but cannot, because their thinking has been deeply altered and damaged. And so, my struggle in writing this story of Uyghurs in concentration camps is twofold. I must grapple with the limitations of linguistic representation and with the challenge of accurately speaking for those who have been stripped of the capacity to think and speak for themselves. I must discuss this horror, advocating for a victim who may not be able to accurately recount and who may even deny their own story.

This is an attempt on my part to begin the process of restoring what is lost, partly or permanently, through the thought reforms and cultural transformation that is taking place in the name of the Chinese public interest. Firstly, I aim to restore the truth about the collective destruction that all Uyghurs in the camps are forced to endure. And secondly, I aim to restore the individual stories of Uyghurs who may have suffered psychological injuries that cause them to misrepresent or negate what has happened.

But there is yet another challenge that arises in my efforts to speak up for Uyghurs in the camps. Where is my credibility, the independent support for the stories I tell? So far, unlike the great Holocaust survivor writers, such as Primo Levi, Elie Wiesel, and others, there are few Uyghurs who have been able to describe the horrors of the camps, and none in great detail. While some Uyghurs have recently been released from the camps into the community, they are under strict conditions not to speak about the experiences they had inside the camp. If these conditions are breached, they are severely punished. Those who have been released are not issued a Chinese passport, so they cannot go abroad to tell their stories in safety. So far, no picture, video, or audio recordings revealing the realities of life inside the camps has emerged, and there have been no witness statements from any workers or camp guards. Very limited information is available; however, the most credible is from the recently leaked Chinese government documents provided to the *New York Times* by Asiye Abdulahad, a Uyghur activist based in the Netherlands. These papers shed unprecedented light on how the CCP mercilessly implemented the harsh crackdown on Uyghurs in East Turkistan. [2]

Another reliable source of information is satellite imagery, which reveals the location and size of existing concentration camps. But satellites, as penetrative as their cameras may be, are unable to record what is happening inside the buildings of the camps. For that level of disclosure, we would need witnesses to be allowed into the facility. However, the only media access allowed in East Turkistan is carefully guided by government officials, showing a highly controlled presentation, and creating a smokescreen to hide the widespread torture inside the camps. According to those in charge, the admission of Uyghurs to the camps is voluntary. The officials will happily show foreign delegates around "re-education centers" where Uyghurs can be seen diligently learning skills essential for their new lives once they return to the community. These camps shown to delegates project the image of a utopia, perfectly belying the dystopian reality.

On this note, there is a certain similarity between the Nazis and CCP and how they mask the reality of the camps, presenting an alternative version to deceive the world. After their request to visit Auschwitz was approved in 1944, the Danish Red Cross and International Red Cross followed a prescribed route that was engineered by the Nazis to portray the Auschwitz camp in the best light possible. The same technique and purpose are at play in the official camp visits organized by the CCP. In both cases, the prisoners were warned how to behave and what to say, and the picture presented bore no resemblance to the daily life prisoners were experiencing. Totalitarian states excel at manipulation of perceptions to distort reality. They use their power to turn a normal, decent, and sane society into an oppressed one, but when checked by external authorities, they know how to turn it back into a "normal" society until those checks are completed. When outsiders are present, the CCP is exceptionally capable of replacing the dystopian reality with a utopian vision. In so doing, it suppresses the truth and convinces the world that this fantasy is the only truth. More significantly, the very act of hiding reality serves ultimately to expose the fact that they demonstrably know the difference between a normal, sane, and healthy society and its opposite. Like the Nazis before them, the CCP know what a normal society looks like, but they are determined to tear it apart mercilessly to create what they claim will be a better one. They are acting on the conviction that their will to purify their society is a historical necessity and a self-justifying duty.

Since 2017, no telephone communication has been allowed between most Uyghurs in exile and Uyghurs inside China. Only those few Uyghurs who are loyal to the CCP can continue to contact their families back home. Most Uyghurs are in a desperate position, not knowing whether their family members are still alive, where their children are, or if they are safe. This is the terror that the CCP has been leveraging to ensure information about the camps is not divulged. As we know from history, the greater the crime, the more secretively it is shrouded. Therefore, these measures are a clear indicator of the seriousness of the crimes being carried out.

In acknowledging I am not a survivor or a firsthand witness to the camps, and I have minimal evidence aside from a few survivor accounts, I must reiterate at the outset that it is dangerous to automatically accept what Chinese ideologists or propagandists are telling us about the camps they euphemistically describe as "re-education centers." These ideologists have repeatedly said the objective of the "re-education centers" is to assist Uyghurs in creating a new life and obtaining professional skills, which could not be further from the truth.

The CCP has been sophisticated in concealing its crime from the world. It is not burning or burying the corpses of Uyghurs on a massive scale as the Nazis did to Jewish people in concentration camps. Instead, it is skillfully erasing the traces of its cruelty through extremely effective measures—for instance, through transferring of Uyghur inmates to remote prisons in different areas in inner China, where nobody knows what is happening to them. There is no seeming justification for these large-scale transfers of Uyghurs to other prisons, not easily observable by satellites, unless it was to erase the traces of the crime.

To write about this hidden and horrific crime is not an easy job. In a situation where you lack sufficient evidence to expose an ongoing crime and defend the lives of innocent victims, where you are ever aware of the clock ticking and with each passing second leaving less time for them to be rescued, you may find yourself indulging in imaginations. The imagination, while it is a great part of any intellectual endeavor, is not suitable for what I am doing here. I am perfectly able to imagine what is happening inside the camps, yet this very imagination serves the interests of the CCP who would like me to succumb to as wild an imagination as possible so that they might undermine or even negate my stories in the end. As such, imagination in this case is a trap. Whatever imagination I attempt to engage myself with, the CCP will be quick to state that what I have told the world is nothing but the sheer fabrication of a dangerous, anti-China writer who intends to sabotage the good intentions of the CCP for Uyghurs.

Sadly, some Uyghur survivors of the genocide may also condemn me for distorting the situation of the camps, accusing me of being too imaginative and hence of being untrustworthy. This response might be not simply the result of Stockholm syndrome, but the product of a long-term and intrusive indoctrination. Inside the camps, not only is there a pattern of deliberate and systematic physical harm of inmates, but there is an ongoing campaign of psychological torture. Their thoughts are mutilated to a level where they are incapacitated, unable to perceive, let alone defend, their own vital or basic interests. Instead, they become a form of talking corpse, praising the torturers and internalizing the blame into their own psyche, saying that they deserve what they have gone through, revealing a profound self-hatred. The camps indoctrinate Uyghurs to hate themselves, guiding them to see that they are sinners who deserve the mortal punishment that is inflicted upon them, while those who truly hate them turn deceivingly into their saviors.

Therefore, all the evidence we can gather from actual witnesses may be useless, for it is distorted beyond recognition, and the causality is inverted. We are confronted with the necessity of bearing indirect witness in such a world, where there is no other means to obtain evidence than by recontextualizing the stories of camp survivors. Nevertheless, while I am aware of these challenges, I aim to write this account as objectively and truthfully as possible, basing my arguments on well-established facts to ensure that it will be credible and convincing. Still, I acknowledge that it will be difficult to convince you as the reader, for the natural way of thinking about such an issue is rather simple: first provide evidence, then analyze, and finally conclude. This is the simple, standardized, and often necessary way of conducting the scientific process. However, the process of finding and documenting evidence takes time, during which the CCP is slowly but surely eliminating Uyghur lives and culture within East Turkistan. Given the secrecy and distortion surrounding it, how much evidence can be enough to guarantee a factual accounting of this matter?

The CCP knows this dilemma well, and it uses it to buy more time to carefully destroy the evidence, leaving the world with few clues about what is happening to Uyghurs. Despite my best efforts to find proof, I know that I will always end up with something too little or too incomplete. Others prefer to disbelieve what a few Uyghur survivors are saying, claiming there is not enough evidence provided to validate the true condition of the camps. The CCP continues to eliminate Uyghurs by controlling the dissemination of information under the protective cloak of this dilemma. Meanwhile, the world justifies its failure to take action under the pretext that the evidence to establish a crime is insufficient, or that the so-called Uyghur crisis is made up by some anti-China politicians in the West, solely to tarnish China's reputation as a great world power.

Even if the world is willing to listen dispassionately to the stories of a few Uyghur survivors, the level of the cruelty the camp guards inflicted upon them is so unimaginable that it almost renders the stories unbelievable. The level of tragedy is so utterly absurd that it almost defies any sense of rational thinking. With awareness and acknowledgment of what has happened to a few, we must consider the reality of what is happening to others in a similar situation on a vast scale. How is it even possible to comprehend, as an example, the Chinese government dispatching almost a million officials, most of whom are Han Chinese, to live and sleep with Uyghurs—mostly women and children—in their homes while their husbands languish in the camps?

Even I, as the storyteller, a deeply rational thinker, find it hard to believe and almost counterintuitive, thanks to its utter absurdity. The whole Uyghur existence is now an absurdity, in fact, defined by the bizarre reality where a killer is a savior, the innocent is a sinner, and the concentration camps are not a killing space, but a learning center. If this is how I feel, even knowing the reality, how am I to convince others? This is the amazing effectiveness of the CCP, which offers the utopic and "rational" perspective, therefore forcing me to support a position that sounds bizarre, absurd, and hostile, despite its veracity. The CCP's hold on the "believable" narrative means its cruelty is easily dismissed, further strengthening its characterization of all condemnation as untrue in the end.

When the mind fails to comprehend, represent, and analyze the information presented, it sometimes resigns itself to silence, relinquishing any interest in further investigation. Confusion paralyzes our thoughts, preventing us from thinking about it further. In short, the horror combined with the absurdity of the Uyghur's situation makes it easy for the CCP to cover up its crimes. I do not mean an existential absurdity, where reason fails to make sense of the repetitive, monotonous, and meaningless nature of life. I am referring to the incomprehensibility of a seemingly civilized nation that is acting on a desire to eliminate an entire group of people in cold blood. The very notion is a direct affront upon and offense against human reasoning and has become a political manipulation to inhibit deeper examination. Within this nullification of reason, where it is now stripped of its critical function, the CCP continues deliberately to kill human thought, and ultimately to kill human life on a massive scale.

In the end, my purpose is to tell the story of a people who have been stripped not only of their right to tell their own story, but of all their human rights. I am writing this as an act of vicarious empowerment, preserving their story so that it is not eradicated from history or taken to the level of silence. Writing is a provocation of memory. Each word of this book bears witness to the story of the people who are forced by a totalitarian regime to be silent and, therefore, forgotten. The ultimate aim of the CCP is to make Uyghurs forget their identity and deny what has happened to them. Perhaps worse yet, it aims to ensure the world has nothing to remember Uyghurs by, leaving them forgotten altogether, as if they never existed. The writing of this book resists this intention; it is an act of rebellious remembrance and an attempt to rescue what has already been and what is about to be lost forever in time. In so doing, it helps restore the collective memories of the victims. Writing is an act of remembrance and commemoration, though this piece inevitably risks becoming bitter, agonizing, and desperate.

Theodor Adorno's famous statement about how to represent the Holocaust still reverberates: "to write poetry after Auschwitz is barbaric."[3] For Adorno, representation of the Holocaust defies any type of categorization, narrative, and expressions, artistic or otherwise. For it had already gone beyond what a form of art could grasp, even poetry—one of the finest forms of art that humanity uses to express their deepest feelings. The intensity of such an unimaginable trauma and irrevocable loss is a rare extreme on the continuum that poetic imagination can visualize, evoke, and describe. Adorno was wary of the possibility that poetry would or could objectify the Holocaust as an ordinary object in the world, or that it would beautify it inadvertently while representing it. And so, the Holocaust, in its unprecedented level of human trauma and suffering, is not representable through literature, according to Adorno. Any attempt to treat it as a mere representation would not only be blasphemy against those who perished but also disrespectful in response to the enormity of the suffering, a pure suffering that no language could fully and faithfully convey.

Now, one might suggest that to write about the Uyghur genocide is equally barbaric, irrespective of what literary form is used. And the task, even if permissible, will be a challenging one. The first issue is that the depth and breadth of the suffering Uyghurs are enduring in the dark corners of concentration camps is too vast to conceptualize. Another issue is that the event is still unfolding and, therefore, it is arguably too early to say anything decisive and conclusive about it. Despite all its deficiencies, subjectivism, and discontentment, history will record how an event started and ended, even while being open to a plurality of narratives. At this point, I have some ideas about how this genocide started but I have no idea how it will end. My vision lacks completeness without a clear ending point to this genocide, one which would allow us to further define its antecedents, based on rules of causality. It is easier to understand an event that is completed, thanks to the benefits of hindsight. Therefore, my main challenge is to write about events currently unfolding with no end in sight, attempting to describe a holistic picture that is still being drawn. I must analyze what is currently happening with very limited information and predict what may happen in the future based on the lessons of history.

In my reflections, the reasoning focuses less on the chronological description of the events, and more on the internal and external impacts of this cruelty and violence. I intend to delve deep into the inner workings of these two factors to make sense of how a state resolves to utterly destroy a people from the inside out, by creating a blanket of apathy. A deafening silence creeps in and engulfs everything, as expressed in the melancholic and ghostly world of Paul Celan's *Todesfuge*, or Death Fugue: "we dig a grave in the breezes there one lies unconfined."[4] For a bystander like me, speaking out is a form of testifying to their experiences, but implies a blasphemy for the fallen people who may not wish to speak of their suffering fully. The trauma creates a bizarre condition where victims believe that it is better to be silent than speaking up. Silence is the absolute demonstration of respect for the deceased victims of violence that is unspeakable. In silence, the gravity of suffering becomes real and authentic, as it creates a condition in which the victims are gone forever. Words cannot restore what is lost permanently; only eternal silence does justice to this eternal loss, from afar with an aura of deep agony.

Afterward, the silence breaks itself suddenly. As Elie Wiesel comments: "In the beginning there was silence—no words. The word itself is a breaking out. The word itself is an act of violence; it breaks the silence. We cannot avoid the silence, we must not. . . . The unspoken is as important as the spoken: the weight of silence is necessary."[5] In this manner, the act of speaking on behalf of the dead and the survivors runs the risk of being construed by them as being complicit in the act of violence. But refraining from speaking is a betrayal of the fallen victims as it follows the demands of the persecutor, who seeks absolute silence over the murders. It is in this resistance against the intention of the persecutor that silence becomes a monument that allows the violence to be unquestioned, rather than challenged and brought to justice. The crime is only highlighted when paying tribute to the dead, whose names may remain unknown forever. The words serve as the epitaph for graves of the victims of genocide, leaving so many dead with no physical remains to mourn or bury.

For a traumatized survivor, maintaining the silence that surrounded the Holocaust was a continuation of the depersonalization tactics used in the Nazi concentration camps. Silence can be corrosive, depressing, and dehumanizing, and is precisely what genocide aims for. It aims to kill the voice, thoughts, and spirits of the victims. It intends to bring everything back to its original state of nothingness. I am striving, not as a survivor, but as a bystander, to break this very silence. I aim to move things from the realm of nothingness to that of being; from the realm of silence to that of words; from the realm of words to that of testimonies, evidence, and judgment. It is a resistance against the terror of nothingness, which defines the absence of language, thoughts, and rationality.

Writing this story is a risky journey. It is not merely recounting or analyzing what is happening to Uyghurs. Nor is it merely an attempt to reconstruct the reality to bring back its dignity. It is about feeling the suffering of Uyghurs at a deeper level. It is an empathetic approach, which risks the writer being ineluctably affected by what is occurring, even to the point of losing one's capacity to speak and reason lucidly. To feel this pain is far more complicated than to simply have knowledge of it, for the latter approach would assist in the objectification of the pain, conceptualizing it theoretically as a self-defense mechanism of sorts. To feel the ongoing genocide intimately and emphatically is a totally different experience. It is a near-death experience. It is feeling like being in the camp with other Uyghurs, even though they cannot sense that you are with them in this emotional solidarity. With its overwhelming vigor and intensity, this experience leaves me feeling at a loss. I am in turmoil, on the brink of an abyss, unable to get back to safety. This book, in this sense, is necessarily as incomplete as the event of this genocide, to show you—the reader—how this violence of the CCP is experienced, not just how it was spoken of.

At the same time, for me, writing is a healing process. During this process, I am prepared to explore and document the darkest aspects of the camps, to portray the horrors of my people's torture, humiliation, and suffering as much as possible, all with the weight of survivor's guilt in my heart. In all this suffering, however, I have not lost hope for discovering a kernel of intrinsic goodness in the hearts of human beings. If I had no trust in this goodness, however small, rare, or insignificant it might be, I would already have resigned myself to absolute despair—I would drop my pen and succumb to utter silence.

The situation of Uyghurs deeply bothers me, making me sleepless most nights. I am suffering with them in spirit, night in and night out. It is not because they are my countrymen, but because they are human beings like any others, none of whom deserve being terrorized and eliminated. This worry propels me to grab a pen to write my reflections about their helpless and hopeless life. The Uyghur genocide is one of the most extreme cases of genocide in human history with its aim, scope, propaganda mechanisms and use of cutting-edge technologies. It forces us to think beyond what we have previously known. It tears apart our emotional comfort and challenges our way of life, centered on our own well-being. It is the greatest challenge to any ethical way of thinking. It is a shameful face of humanity, and I am calling for the world to end its silence, as I am doing, here and now.

NOTES

1. Elie Wiesel, Lucy Dawidowicz, Dorothy Rabinowitz, and Robert McAfee Brown, *Dimensions of the Holocaust* (Evanston: Northwestern University Press, 1990), 7.

2. Austin Ramzy and Chris Buckley. "'Absolutely No Mercy': Leaked Files Expose How China Organized Mass Detentions of Muslims," *New York Times*, November 16, 2019, https://www.nytimes.com/interactive/2019/11/16/world/asia/china-xinjiang-documents.html.

3. Anna-Verena Nosthoff, "Barbarism: Notes on the Thought of Theodor W. Adorno," Critical Legal Thinking, October 15, 2014, https://criticallegalthinking.com/2014/10/15/barbarism-notes-thought-theodor-w-adorno/.

4. Alan Rosen (ed.), *Literature of the Holocaust* (Cambridge: Cambridge University Press, 2013), 6.

5. Heidi Anne Walker, "How and Why I Write: Interview with Wiesel," *Journal of Education*, vol. 2, 119, Boston University, 1980.

Chapter Two

From Oblivion to Exposure

In 2018, I came across a government document that explained the strategy used by the CCP to destroy the Uyghurs' most primordial familial and cultural connections at the deepest level possible, and thus surrender them to their will. This internal CCP document reported by news agency AFP stated the aim of the camps holding Uyghurs and other Turkic Muslims was to "break their lineage, break their roots, break their connections, and break their origins."[1] In Chinese, this is called the resolute implementation of the Four Breaks (坚决落实"四断"，做到断代，断根，断联，断源), in the fight against the two-faced people (两面派). These Four Breaks are actually the expression of another Chinese proverb, one which gets to the heart of the issue: "to break the roots to make it extinct" (断根绝种). As a *Washington Post* editorial recently concluded, "It's hard to read that as anything other than a declaration of genocidal intent."[2] I begin my reflections with this revelation, demonstrating the intent of the CCP to eliminate Uyghurs. As we continue, I will explore throughout the book how this intention is implemented—thoroughly, deeply, and mercilessly.

The horrors of the Holocaust are most often visually illuminated with photos of Jewish people in striped pajamas, in Nazi concentration camps, looking profoundly sad, tired, and terrified. The visual representations of the Uyghur genocide, however, are largely devoid of human life. They are, first and foremost, characterized by the photos of hidden buildings with high barbed-wire fences, surrounded by police guards. Within the walls of these buildings, widespread torture, humiliation, rape, organ harvesting, forced labor, and death happen daily, according to statements from survivors. As the number of victim statements given by Uyghurs and Kazakhs grew, and as media articles were published about them, these images have sunk deep into our collective unconsciousness. Initially, we were in disbelief and denial;

however, we have now started painfully to swallow the toxic truth about the reality of the camps.

No one who has seen these images will ever forget them in their frightening shape, color, and location; they will haunt us from generation to generation. They will define, implicitly and explicitly, the contents of our nightmares, aspirations, and identity, over which we struggle to retain control. The invasion of these thoughts into our mind feels as unstoppable as the invasion of the Chinese Liberation Army into our homeland, East Turkistan, in 1949, which changed our reality forever.

These images of concentration camps form a spatial awareness vacuum in our minds, an area of terrifying nothingness. They provoke visions of desperate-looking children behind bars, after being separated from their parents who are incarcerated in concentration camps or in prisons, under the ubiquitous surveillance cameras that proliferate both inside and outside of the camps. They are profoundly eerie and depressingly silent buildings where an increasing number of chilling crimes are perpetrated in darkness. As more images of the concentration camps surfaced, slowly but surely, the world became aware that the CCP has created one of the world's most horrific new Gulags. Across East Turkistan and other parts of inner China, they are incarcerating Uyghurs, Kazakhs, and other Turkic and non-Turkic Muslims with a sweeping determination to destroy their lives.

Omir Bekali, a Kazakh national, was one of the first victims to speak out publicly about his experience in a camp in East Turkistan. He exposed the horrific situation he faced within the concentration camps in his talks with Gerry Shih of AP News, which were then shared in an article titled "China's mass indoctrination camps invoke Cultural Revolution."[3] In his testimony, he stated that "The psychological pressure is enormous, when you have to criticize yourself, denounce your thinking, your own ethnic group. . . . I still think about it every night, until the sun rises. I can't sleep. The thoughts are still with me."

Adrian Zenz, a senior fellow in China Studies at the Victims of Communism Memorial Foundation in Washington, DC, along with other researchers, conducted critical research on the hidden corners of the Chinese internet. By analyzing a trail of seventy-three government procurement and construction bids valued at nearly 700 billion RMB (approximately 108 million USD), he uncovered evidence of a security buildup in East Turkistan, with budget plans and other documents that illuminated what this gigantic infrastructure means for Uyghurs. As a result of his research, he estimated the number of detainees in internment camps "could be closer to 1.1 million, which equates to 10–11 percent of the adult Muslim population of the region."[4] Zenz recently told Radio Free Asia that "China has built more than 1,000 internment camps for ethnic Uyghurs and other Muslims in the Xinjiang Uyghur Autonomous Region (XUAR)."[5] Recent satellite images corroborate this claim. In particular, new satellite imagery collated and analyzed by the Australian Strategic Policy Institute think tank identified the rapid expansion of twenty-eight detention camps with more than 2 million square meters in November 2018.[6]

In addition to the construction of new internment camp facilities, efforts to upgrade and expand existing facilities have been documented. In many cases, public schools, manufacturing plants, and other facilities have been repurposed as internment camps.[7] These shocking results were immediately bolstered by the United Nations, claiming that it has "credible reports that China holds a million Uyghurs in secret camps."[8] The US government accused China of incarcerating more than one million Uyghurs in the concentration camps in the strongest US condemnation to date: The United States estimates that since April 2017, China has detained more than one million Muslim men, women and children in forced labor camps. Up to two million more have been sent for political indoctrination in daytime facilities. All told, the number of Chinese citizens in these facilities constitutes some 15 to 25 percent of Xinjiang's total ethnic-minority population. The U.S. Congressional-Executive Commission on China described the situation as the largest mass incarceration of a minority population in the world today."[9]

The revelations of the camps offered a new, shocking paradigm change towards the treatment of Uyghurs by China. The world had been awakened to the nightmarish nature of the Chinese Dream introduced by Xi Jinping. In a plurality of articles, TV programs, and panel discussions, people were gradually coming to terms with the horrific reality faced by Uyghurs.

With this growing weight of evidence, the CCP has been under pressure to respond to reports of the secret elimination of Uyghurs in these camps. When they finally broke their silence, they did not deny the existence of the camps but portrayed them very differently, positioning them as merely "re-education centers" where Uyghurs and Kazaks are offered training to improve their life skills, to learn Mandarin and Chinese law.

For us, this paradoxical propaganda came as an emotional tsunami, overwhelmingly threatening our sense of reality and hope for the future. Suddenly, the CCP, previously perceived by many Uyghurs as a benevolent and just party, was revealed to be a monster, forcibly seizing Uyghurs who would then disappear into the black hole of the concentration camps. First overwhelmed by shock, then gripped with disbelief, and finally consumed by depression, we went through a destabilizing period of emotional turbulence. We were left broken deep inside by this twofold cause: Firstly, the enormity of the sheer, indescribable cruelty that the CCP has inflicted upon our compatriots in East Turkistan. Secondly, and more fundamentally, the shattering of our previous idealistic and naïve conviction that the world would come to our aid once the depth and scale of this atrocity was revealed.

Some Uyghurs still are not convinced that the CCP would be deliberately murderous. They cannot conceive of a body they once trusted now being intent on wiping them off the face of the earth with vicious determination, calculation, and political zeal. Some remain under the illusion that Uyghurs might still live harmoniously with Han Chinese while repeating the government rhetoric of loving the CCP. They also believe that as long as they do not participate in what is known as the Three Evils[10] (terrorism, separatism, and religious extremism), they will have no problem with the CCP. The indiscriminate nature of internment of Uyghurs has sent an alarming message to Uyghurs in exile. The arrest and punishment of former governor of Xinjiang, Nur Bekri, has provided an example for how sweeping the crackdown on Uyghurs in East Turkistan really is. He was once commonly referred to as "Nöl Bekri," a play on his name meaning "Zero Bekri" in Uyghur language. He was seen as a lame duck in the high echelons of the Chinese-led political system, who defended the elimination of Uyghur language from all levels of education. His arrest and punishment were shocking news for us. It became clear that no Uyghur is safe in China.

The collective shock was not only due to how Nur Bekri and other senior Uyghur officials have been removed from their posts one by one. It was also clear that the criteria used to justify arresting or punishing Uyghurs was becoming more nebulous. Now, the level of loyalty a Uyghur shows to the CCP has become irrelevant. Everyone is at risk of being taken into a camp eventually. For Uyghurs within China, being put in a camp is only a matter of time, not of probability. It has become overwhelmingly clear that as long as your ethnic identity is that of a Uyghur at best and a Muslim at worst, the CCP considers you a target for elimination. Uyghurs, as a unique people, are the target; all else is just a footnote.

Despite chilling revelations that the CCP shows no mercy for Uyghurs, regardless of their political or religious affiliations, some Uyghurs in exile are still reluctant to make a public statement about the whereabouts of their relatives in the camps. They have had no communication with them for the past few years out of fears for the safety of their families and, in some cases, their own safety. This lucid, painful awareness has not resulted in massive campaigns, organized by Uyghurs in exile, against the inhuman practices of the CCP in East Turkistan. Instead, their reaction is depressingly slow, ill-coordinated, and ineffective, and the failure to mount a more significant organized response has two causes.

Firstly, some still believe the CCP might reverse its treatment of Uyghurs under pressure from the international community. They still hope that it might return to its "benign" governance of Uyghurs, as was the case before. With this slim hope, these Uyghurs have preferred to be silent to avoid irritating the CCP, because to do so would worsen the volatile situation for their family and friends, both inside the camps and outside living in East

Turkistan. Silence is a calculated response to the widespread, unprecedented state-sponsored violence against Uyghurs, based on the optimistic but misguided assumption that the CCP is intrinsically good-natured. In their minds, what the CCP is doing to Uyghurs must be just a temporary mistake. Their understanding can not admit the unfortunate reality that the CCP is determined to eliminate everybody indiscriminately, whether loyal to the CCP interest or not. A deeper look at this attitude shows that a survivalist mentality, driven by fear, has taken on the form of loyalty among these Uyghurs. They are now ready to justify any violence the CCP may resort to, so long as it does not kill them personally. This sense of fear has been well-captured in the following quote from a news article:

> Two months ago the UN and EU did some inspections in the region [Xinjiang], and my city was chosen for these inspections, and I heard they released a lot of people because they [China] want to hide what they're doing to Uyghurs, and my mother could be one of the released, but I can't confirm if the news is true because I don't want to risk trying to contact her because they [Chinese authorities] will detain and torture her again or worse.[11]

Secondly, Uyghurs are disinclined to speak out because of an attitude they have been forced to internalize over the decades, through thought transformations, which has resulted in a sophisticated and effective level of mental self-censorship. They have been guided by this process to accept and believe that they ought to be obedient, faithful, and compliant to the CCP, which is so powerful that it can crush any Uyghur dissent. This thought process is so deeply ingrained that they believe only the CCP can decide who is to cherish and who is to perish. As a result, consciously or unconsciously, this thought process diminishes their courage to the point that they cannot speak up against the CCP.

In addition to these fears creating a sense of deepening silence among some Uyghurs in exile at the beginning, the silence of the rest of the world over the killing of Uyghurs had left us with mixed reactions. Some felt abandoned and betrayed as they thought their rights would be defended by the world, however general or abstract this term may sound. For others, their silence over the atrocities of the CCP is justified in and by the silence of the world. Both forms of silence insinuate there is consideration that it is wise not to play with fire; otherwise, the costs of the CCP's retaliation would be too disastrous to sustain.

Silence is perceived as a protective strategy for both Uyghurs in exile and at home in China, to avoid being targeted by the CCP. Unfortunately, in the end, it has failed to protect us from being exposed to collective trauma, irrespective of our political or religious affiliations. Although there is no comprehensive research on this subject, it is still possible to observe the Uyghur diaspora communities across the globe that have been exposed to this very trauma in varying degrees. Many Uyghurs have described to me being overwhelmed by episodes of fear, anxiety, and depression, the combination of which is the manifestation of collective trauma, invisibly but rapidly spreading amongst them at home, in the local communities, and internationally.

On the other hand, generally, the indifference of the world to our desperate plight has added to our trauma. Sadly and shockingly, the lack of response to the Uyghur crisis bears a remote resemblance to the atmosphere of the camps, where camp guards suppress the voices of inmates. They are forced to be silent and are silenced forever. We have not experienced a world that is caring and graceful as we naively believed. On the contrary, we have painfully discovered the attitude of this world, which appears to us as weak, indifferent, and stonehearted. This is almost more painful than our discovery of the truth about the camps themselves. Again, we are reminded miserably of the attitude of Chinese guards in the camps, who are also indifferent to the crying of Uyghurs, Kazakhs, and other inmates, as they are subject to unbearable torture. We have been thrown into a pit of despair, feeling worthless, abandoned, and cursed. We feel as if we are fated to a life of suffering, longing for what we could never have, deserve, and cherish. The resulting level of self-abandonment amplifies our self-pity, agony, and sense of powerlessness. We have resigned ourselves to face this impossible situation, the indifference, and the inhumanity.

Hence, we find ourselves deeply immersed in confusion, awakening to a cold reality and realization that we are alone, left to our own devices to deal with our loss, sorrows, and trauma. We feel hopeless and helpless; we are depressed and traumatized in a way that is similar to the emotional experience of our compatriots in the camps. We are experiencing collective trauma, as to be sensitive to the effects of the traumatic event is a natural human reaction to it.

Uyghurs have long been unknown, a stranger to the world, but now they are renowned as one of the worst-persecuted peoples. Their stories are analyzed differently from one source to another, and they have been given a host of names. We have been called Uyghur Muslims, Uighurs, the Muslim minority, or even Chinese Muslims, in some media articles. The plurality of proper names ascribed to us indicates that we are not clearly recognized in the way we prefer to be identified.

However, this is not how Uyghurs were initially introduced to the collective consciousness of people around the world. The first time Uyghurs saw the spotlight was in a historic moment after the 9/11 terrorist attacks, which propelled the US invasion in Afghanistan. At that time, in Afghanistan and Pakistan, some Uyghurs were captured for being on the terrorist enemy line, and their identity as Uyghurs was widely cited by news outlets. These Uyghurs were later detained in Guantanamo Bay. After their eventual release, they successfully sought protection in several countries including Bermuda, Albania, Palau, and Switzerland. The stories of Guantanamo Bay Uyghurs brought this hitherto unknown people into the limelight, identifying them as a people who aligned themselves with Al-Qaida to fight against the US as terrorists.

The CCP have since used the identity of a few Uyghurs, accused of being aligned with terrorism, to tarnish the identity of Uyghurs as a collective people. They are portrayed as a hidden enemy of the state and as part of a global terrorist network. The CCP have further branded Uyghurs as separatists by propagating reports of incidents involving a small number of Uyghurs in Tiananmen Square, the Kunming Train Station incidents, and the Urumqi riot. This false image of Uyghurs has been widely and wildly cited by the CCP to demonize Uyghurs, portraying them as people with an innate tendency towards terrorism.

But if this clamping down on all Uyghurs is a valid response to a generic threat of terrorism, then why not apply it all around the globe, collectively painting every Muslim as a terrorist who must be eliminated? Obviously, because to do so would be a devastating discriminatory reaction, breeding hatred, provoking violence, and ultimately playing into the hands of terrorists. So, why is the CCP an exception to this rule? Must I point out the irony of justifying genocide as a fight against terrorism? Further, may I ask which of the two is more evil? Both genocide and terrorism are evil, equally barbaric, and historically not tolerated by the world. So, why does the latter incite an armed response from the US and its allies, and the former does not?

Now Uyghurs are known in many parts of the world for tragic reasons: a people going through ethnic cleansing, or cultural genocide, or religious persecution, depending on your perspective on the issue. For a credulous mind, if Uyghurs are seen collectively as terrorists and separatists, then it becomes difficult to question the behavior of the CCP when they choose to put them in camps. If these people are dangerous and unpredictable, then they ought to be disciplined and prevented from destroying social harmony and stability any further. This political "logic" aims to realign the traditional boundary of good and evil, for it is a categorical imperative to eliminate any threat to China—real or potential—indiscriminately and without hesitation. Political practicality is the key. Within this context, the CCP have tacitly established a plausible justification for eliminating Uyghurs, whose presence in society poses a threat to China's safety. Arguably, they must be isolated from the Chinese population by being incarcerated and the threat contained. This is a radical form of an apartheid system, segregating Uyghurs from the rest of society. As such, we have lost our rightful position as the natural inhabitants of the land we claim as our ancestral land.

For us, to be known by the world as victims of genocide seems excessive. We were not prepared to be viewed in such an intense and even radical way.

Our identity is still under negotiation with the CCP, the world, and ourselves. It is a multi-layered identity and needs to be packaged into a unified format that reflects our cultural uniqueness, current reality, and potential future. Primarily, Uyghurs identify themselves with their ancestry as a Turkic people, being part of the broader network of Turkistan, covering the Central Asian region and beyond. As a largely Muslim people, we are part of the global Muslim community. However, as compulsory Chinese citizens, we are legally bound to obey the CCP at the expense of compromising on and potentially losing our identity.

The challenge for Uyghurs has been attempting to integrate their ancestral Turkic identity with that of Han Chinese. This integration is difficult, given the inevitable clashes of a majority Islamic culture existing within the dominant, fiercely secular Han Chinese culture. Moreover, having Uyghurs maintain a Turkic identity is not ideal for the CCP, as it provides a stark reminder to the world of the Chinese invasion of East Turkistan in 1949. Despite this, Uyghurs have attempted to bring these two cultural identities into coexistence, in furtherance of their political, religious, and cultural survival. However, the Uyghur genocide has revealed cracks in this combined identity. The CCP has taken advantage of this fragmentation to punish its Uyghur "citizens" by portraying their tendency to terrorism as a Turkic people. The specter of Turkic Muslim Uyghurs threatening the national interest of China by attempting to recreate the East Turkistan Islamic Republics is a potent purveyor of fear to the Han Chinese masses.

In reality, Uyghurs are a people in between. We are not Chinese enough to be spared the wrath of China, which aims to assimilate us at all costs as an anomaly in the great Middle Kingdom (中国). We are also not Muslim enough for the hard-liner Arab Muslims, who have not come to save us from the oppression of the infidels as instructed in the Qur'an. And we are not Turkish enough for devout Turkish nationalists, who fail to defend our rights under the guidance of the nationalistic slogan of *"Ne mutlu Türküm diyene"* ("How proud to say that I am a Turk"). Uyghurs are a people by half in any measure, be it political, religious, or cultural. The paradox of our identity is that we are Chinese citizens as Muslims in an atheistic regime, all while maintaining our cultural identity as a Turkic nation. Taken separately, none of these individual characteristics identifies us fully in the end. Nor does the CCP allow the combination of this identity further as it is incompatible with its nation-state building process. As a result, Uyghurs' identity is ambiguous in the strictest sense of the word: we are, strictly speaking, political nobodies in the guise of cultural somebodies.

We find ourselves at the center of the world's attention, not as an ancient people with a glorious past, but as a modern people becoming extinct. It is not clear to us why we are punished so harshly, or why the world is so oblivious to our suffering. Being confronted with the lack of interest and attention from the rest of the world is as burdensome as it is problematic. As a people, we were not psychologically prepared to orient ourselves within this new arena, dealing with the world's myriad conflicting emotional reactions that range from hatred and apathy to sympathy and compassion. At the same time, we recognize that we are on the world stage and must perform the role ascribed to us as victims of one of the worst human rights crises of the twenty-first century. It is as if we are an object being discovered by others in an awkward and shameful situation, unable to hide our vulnerability.

Our emotional responses to this unfolding genocide have also revealed the complex layers of our existential orientation in this world. They have shaped the meaning of our existence. Our experiences have revealed the darkest and brightest parts in us, under the shadow of death and in the midst of a struggle for survival. In an astonishing and contradictory way, the threat to our existence both destroys yet simultaneously sparks within us the desire for life, for the preservation of our culture, for survival, and, above all, for being human. As such, we have each experienced the whole gamut of being a human in a crisis. What we have learned is, you can kill a man, but not his spirit—which is divine and everlasting.

NOTES

1. Louisa Lim, "China: reengineering the Uighur," The Interpreter, Lowy Institute, November 7, 2018, https://www.lowyinstitute.org/the-interpreter/China-re-engineer-uighur.

2. Henryk Szadziewski, "Disappeared forever?" China Channel, February 28, 2019, https://chinachannel.org/2019/02/21/uighur-eliticide/.

3. Gerry Shih, "China's mass indoctrination camps evoke Cultural Revolution," AP News, Associated Press, May 18, 2018, https://www.apnews.com/6e151296f b194f85ba69a8babd972e4b.

4. "The Uyghur men jailed in mass arrests in Xinjiang," AsiaNews, June 19, 2018, http://www.asianews.it/news-en/Uyghur-men-jailed-in-mass-arrests-in-Xinjiang-44210.html

5. Alim Seytoff and Joshua Lipes, "Expert Estimates China Has More Than 1000 Internment Camps For Xinjiang Uyghurs," Radio Free Asia, November 13, 2019.

6. Mark Doman, Stephen Hutcheon, Dylan Welch and Kyle Taylor, "China's Frontier of Fear," ABC News, November 1, 2018, https://www.abc.net.au/news/2018-11-01/satellite-images-expose-chinas-network-of-re-education-camps/10432924.

7. "China's 21st Century Internment Camps in the Uyghur Region," International Uyghur Human Rights & Democracy Foundation, August 20, 2018, http://www.iuhrdf.org/content/china's-21st-century-internment-camps-uyghur-region.

8. Stephanie Nebehay, "U.N. Says It Has Credible Reports That China Holds Million Uighurs in Secret Camps," Reuters, August 12, 2018, https://www.reuters.com/article/us-china-rights-un/u-n-says-it-has-credible-reports-that-china-holds-million-uighurs-in-secret-camps-idUSKBN1KV1SU.

9. Nathan Sales and Sam Brownback, "Opinion: China's Attack on Uighurs Isn't Counterterrorism. It's Ugly Repression," *Washington Post*, May 22, 2019, https://www.washingtonpost.com/opinions/chinas-attack-on-uighurs-isnt-counterterrorism-its-ugly-repression/2019/05/22/7bfb1d60-7ccb-11e9-a5b3-34f3edf1351e_story.html.

10. The phrase is frequently used when referring to counterterrorism operations undertaken by China, the Central Asian republics, and Russia in the wider context of the Shanghai Cooperation Organization. This term resonates remotely with the notion of the Three Evils in Bud-

dhism. As such, it appeals to deep religious feelings of the Han Chinese (who have a splendid tradition of Buddhism) against the Uyghurs as part of this category, albeit indirectly.

11. CJ Werleman, "How Uyghurs Are Silenced from Sharing Their Suffering with the World," TRT World, May 14, 2019, https://www.trtworld.com/opinion/how-uyghurs-are-silenced-from-sharing-their-suffering-with-the-world-26636.

Chapter Three

Four Modalities of Being Uyghur

In the beginning, this genocide was a surreal and otherworldly event for us. We had neither conceptual schema to understand it fully, nor any awareness of the true level of existential threat in the situation we were collectively facing. As time went by, we became suffused with the feeling, as in a nightmare, of sinking deeper and deeper into quicksand without knowing how far down we were going. It was as if we had been forcibly plunged into a bottomless abyss, and we might never again be able to surge to the surface of our collective consciousness. Death ceased to be a terminating or annihilating force, becoming instead something we experienced repeatedly, without ever attaining the release of an actual, physical death. There was no foreseeable end to the torment of this lucid, sharp, and overwhelming awareness. This experience has, therefore, altered the modalities of our being in the world, irrevocably and fundamentally.

We had all been living in a comfort zone of sorts, brought forcefully out of it upon receiving the tragic news of families, friends, and others imprisoned in the CCP's "re-education camps." We reached out to the world to help us deal with the effects of this massive displacement of Uyghurs, the forced separation from their homes, children, neighborhoods, and towns as they were taken into the camps. In the process, we emerged from our private zone, forced into the public zone—seeking help, sympathy, and compassion from strangers. In experiencing this genocide within these two zones, we have developed four common modalities of being a Uyghur in this world: fatalism, shame, guilt, and helplessness.

FATALISM

Let us begin with the mode of fatalism, a defining mode of our existence, wherein we experience the inescapability of our situation as fate. More deeply, it is a mode ineluctably entangled with our overall identity and existence, despite our being constantly monitored by a surveillance state within our motherland. It is also a way of entrapping us in our history, present reality, and dreams. Ultimately, it is at the heart of the very definition of being a Uyghur—a cultural identity choosing us before we chose it.

Turkish fatalism (or *kismet* in Turkish), a concept described by Nietzsche in his book *The Wanderer and His Shadow*, refers to an attitude of resignation when facing events thought to be inevitable: "The fatalism of the Turk has this fundamental defect, that it contrasts man and fate as two distinct things. Man, says this doctrine, may struggle against fate and try to baffle it, but in the end fate will always gain the victory. Hence the most rational course is to resign oneself or to live as one pleases. As a matter of fact, every man is himself a piece of fate."[1]

It is acceptance of the unavoidable and hence unchangeable, regardless of any action endeavoring to resolve it. As part of our Turkish heritage, the Uyghur identity has always encapsulated and manifested this fatalistic tendency, and it is more prominent than ever in the midst of this genocide. Nietzsche identifies kismet (or fate) as the Turkish people's definition of and explanation for unexpected, unexplainable, or coincidental misfortune. Kismet is a simple, commonly accepted explanation of the inexplicable, intended to encourage people to reconcile with adversity. It does not signify the resignation of one's power to the inevitable, or a higher power, or a god. It is not defeatism, nor is it a belief in some esoteric or mystic way beyond the comprehension of the human mind. Rather, it is an acknowledgment that we live in a world ruled by fate. In essence, it is an attitude of embracing one's pre-determined situation in this world, and within this context I will analyze the case of Uyghurs.

To be a Uyghur in mainstream Chinese society is a daily challenge. Biologically speaking, the faces of Uyghurs are characteristically distinct from those of Han Chinese. This visible difference is deeply political, as difference is perceived as otherness, alterity, or worse, a threat; it must be domesticated in a same way that a foreign (proper) name is pronounced in a Chinese way. Moreover, it carries negative connotations of being politically dangerous, psychologically unpredictable, and fanatically religious. Anyone whose face bears the classic Uyghur features is easily recognizable and targeted as problematic. For example, having a beard is currently incompatible with the dress code, so those Uyghurs who have beards are seen as threatening to Han Chinese society. In ancient China, the beard was considered to be a sign of wisdom, maturity, and social status, depending on its size and shape. However, in modern China, the beard is no longer common, as Lin Yutang states, "A study of the hair and skin of the people also seems to indicate what must be considered results of millenniums of civilized indoor living. The general lack or extreme paucity of beard on man's face is one instance of such effect, a fact which makes it possible for most Chinese men not to know the use of a personal razor."[2]

After the establishment of the People's Republic of China, the beard was seen as part of the Four Olds of the old tradition (i.e., old customs, culture, habit, and ideas), which were abandoned during the Cultural Revolution. To be bearded is no longer a socially and culturally encouraged behavior, even though many ideological fathers of Communism had long beards, including Karl Marx, Friedrich Engels, and Lenin. Earlier in their lives, both Mao Zedong and Zhou Enlai sported long beards, but each shaved it off to establish an image of uniformity and comradeship. Now, Han Chinese society finds it hard to tolerate diverse facial hair features.

Uyghurs have maintained their ironically similar ancient cultural tradition of leaving a beard with Han Chinese as a sign of social status, wisdom, and maturity, which has led to a disparity with the modern Han Chinese culture under the CCP. More importantly, Uyghurs consider it an aesthetic sign of masculinity. Recently, the CCP has mounted a strong challenge against this Uyghur cultural tradition. In 2017, an official dress code restricted the growth and display of a Uyghur long beard in public spaces in East Turkistan.[3] The CCP justified the measure within the context of anti-terrorism, which assumes that displaying a long beard is an overt sign of religious attitude, or religious defiance, against the secular socio-political order. Punishment for such a crime consists of confinement to a concentration camp for "re-education."

This response seems unnecessary and extreme in a society that is already fully equipped to monitor the behavior of Uyghurs through its omnipresent security cameras. With these lenses, the CCP tracks and observes Uyghurs anywhere, anytime, and for any reason. Under this scrutiny, Uyghurs are made highly visible, and any Uyghur "threat" is easily traceable and manageable. Paradoxically, this new measure for attempting to restrict Uyghur beards seems to undermine the clear intentions of the CCP. Instead of restricting beards, they should have encouraged Uyghurs to leave them, thus making their true, threatening nature all the more visible to the omnipresent cameras.

This apparent contradiction illustrates that the Han Chinese fear of a Uyghur beard runs deeper than aesthetic differences and political ideology. The visible beards of Uyghurs can be easily and directly associated with their religious and cultural identity, seen as a direct threat to the cultural homogeneity of the Han Chinese. In the post-9/11 world, the media—in newspapers, books, and cartoons—have tacitly agreed on a consistent representation of

Muslims with three key objects: religious dress, a beard, and a sword. The religious dress is symbolic of their religious identity, the beard implies a frightening and aggressive personality, and a sword represents the perceived violent nature of their faith. This image has been successfully ingrained within Han Chinese psyche at both a conscious and sub-consciousness level and has cemented the notion that a beard is a sign of a threat.

Many Uyghurs believe the nomadic people of the Hunnic Empire, who lived outside of the Great Wall in the north and west of ancient China, are their ancestral forebears. The Huns frequently invaded inland China and were regarded as an enemy. The Chinese called them *Xiongnu* (匈奴), meaning barbarian, savage, or foreign slave. Linguistically, this name captures the conflicting feelings the Chinese had towards the ancient Huns. Fear of the rebellious and untamable barbarians coexisted with a perception of them as already-tamed slaves. Politically speaking, this expression of political rivalry and enmity through a linguistic expression was an attempt to syntactically restructure the world, peoples, natural objects, and feelings. More than simply a communicative tool, language for Han Chinese is a political tool to ascribe underlying meaning, including relationships, interests, status, and goals. It creates a political reality and a reference point in the sense that the name given to the Huns provides a timeless political identity, a clearly demarcated "us vs. them" dichotomy. It also identifies a developing master-and-slave relationship, where Han Chinese became the master and Huns—and ultimately Uyghurs—became the slaves.

The Han Chinese saw the Huns, above all other peoples, as their fiercest and deadliest enemy. The Huns threatened to destroy them altogether many times throughout history. Therefore, the fear of the nomadic Huns went deep into the Han Chinese collective unconsciousness. The ancient politicians of the Middle Kingdom were defenders of a civilization that imagined itself at the center of the world, the center of order, power, and prosperity, and had started to take the security of its borders seriously. Historically, to the Chinese consciousness, the periphery of China was a space of chaos, violence, and barbarism. Emperor Wu, the seventh emperor of the Han dynasty, declared war against the Huns and ultimately defeated them. From then on, Han descendants no longer needed to appease and bribe a barbarian race, which they had found deeply humiliating. This victory had finally freed them from an enduring fear of the Huns.

Chinese politicians managed to put an end to the age-old threat of the Huns through dogged determination. The success came through calm, savvy diplomacy, soft approaches, and the strategic thoroughness of Chinese politicians. Though the Huns were ultimately defeated, Han Chinese never forgot their bloody history with them, and in their minds, the Huns remained a vicious and untamable enemy. The linguistic use of the same name for the Huns today evokes the same psychological reactions as it did more than two thousand years ago. Currently, Uyghurs—as putative descendants of the Huns—and other nomadic and city dwellers in the Tarim Basin, are a historical unconscious reminder for Han Chinese. There is a deep-seated and ancient fear, hatred, and animosity towards Uyghurs.

The treatment of Uyghurs in East Turkistan is a continuation of these ancient conflicts, imagined or real. Any Uyghur with a beard evokes this ancient perception of the Hunnic threat, blended with their contemporary religious identity as Muslims. The image of an ancient, bearded barbarian has been blended into and revived by the post-modern image of the bearded terrorist. The identity of Uyghurs as both Hunnic and Muslims bolsters this image in a new political reality. By their ancestral association, they will pay a historical debt doubled with the current one, which is too politically costly for them.

The relationship between the Chinese and Uyghur cultures is historical, political, and cultural. Thus, it is pre-definable as political kismet. They live together in a deterministic world, not scientifically, but culturally speaking. Uyghurs still live in this nightmarish history, as if the work of historical determination that put them in direct conflict with Han Chinese is still ongoing. At that time in history when this began, neither Uyghurs nor Han Chinese were known as such. Their historical perceptions of each other are strangely interconnected, and they have been recharged anew in the course of recent events, defying the passage of more than 2000 years.

In the current manifestation of this historical confrontation, Han Chinese are placing Uyghurs in concentration camps. This is another variation on the Uyghurs' eternal political kismet, as they are culturally oppressed and forced to either become Han Chinese or be destroyed by them. Security cameras are everywhere, reinforcing this historical inescapability. It is a horrific, intrusive world living under the gaze of Big Brother, a dystopian world where Uyghurs' movements are traced precisely on grids of space and time. This unavoidable exposure is a complete invasion of their personal space, depriving them of privacy, and forcing them to live out their lives in a public space with nowhere to hide. In such a world, Uyghurs have lost their right to be invisible to others, and most importantly, to the CCP. Under surveillance of the CCP, each Uyghur is forced to realize that they are no longer a private person but a public one, brutally stripped of their ability to feel safe. Instead, they feel stalked, observed, and objectified in their own world.

For Uyghurs, this surveillance is the initial stage of exposing vulnerability and creating a mindset of loss of power over their personal lives. Once detained in the camps, phase two begins. Individuals are subject to torture, rape, organ harvesting, slave labor, and death, without any right or ability to defend themselves. They lose their capacity to protect their bodies against indiscriminate violence, inflicted at any time and for any reason. Their bodies are the first things destroyed. Then, their mind is targeted, as it is the only remaining area where the last sanctuary of privacy lies. The mind, like the body of the inmate, must also be ruthlessly invaded and violated, until it, too, is exposed through confessions, incantations, brainwashing, and self-criticism, as Mr. Bekali described. The violence continues until the inmate's inner thoughts are revealed, and the fully exposed human is objectified, emptied, castrated, and disempowered. After this treatment, inmates become a blank canvas in a vegetative state.

The CCP has finally realized their ancient desire to reduce Uyghurs to nothing. The blank canvas they produce through torture is then painted with a different picture, one that suits the purposes of the CCP, and can be destroyed once it is no longer useful. The realization of this goal could liberate Han Chinese forever from the suppressed fear and anxiety in their hearts. They have successfully defeated, deformed, and destroyed Uyghurs, and can now declare that they are less than human. After more than two millennia, Uyghurs have finally been returned to where they belong, back to nature, to being "primal" and "uncivilized," reduced to a state that is more animal than human.

While there is torture inside of the camps, the life of Uyghurs outside is equally horrific. Despite the CCP's claim that they have freedom of movement, it feels to Uyghurs as if they are already inside the walls of the camps. They live under constant surveillance from security cameras and are subject to random checks not applicable to Han Chinese citizens. Under this intense scrutiny, instead of feeling safe, Uyghurs feel threatened and confused. Living with no clear benchmark of acceptable behavior, anything they do could place them in a camp. They are forced to accept how dangerous they are and why they are so rightly scrutinized. The surveillance is so intense that they are even afraid to seek refuge in their inner thoughts, fearing that some technological advance may lay bare their minds and transfer the contents to the police. To have a distinct and unique thought is as dangerous as wearing a long beard in such a reality.

SHAME

Under such inescapable duress, Uyghurs often feel a compelling urge to disappear into their souls, leaving their body behind them as a mere shell in human shape that confirms their existence. Unfortunately, there is no such escape from the body, as Plato describes it: the soul is imprisoned in the body.[4] The Uyghurs' bodies, in turn, are imprisoned within that hostile society. Hence, logically speaking, Uyghurs' souls are imprisoned in this society. Thus imprisoned, even when not in a camp, a soul will gradually wither away due to fear, anxiety, and depression. It is a gradual process of dying, accompanied by a cognitive process of struggling to understand why they are left alive, despite feeling as if they are already dead. This is a shameful life, a life led in the midst of daily humiliation.

For Sartre, shame is an existential mode that defines an intersubjective interaction between the self and the other, revealing our exposure and vulnerability. At the core of this mode lies a futile attempt to deny one's unfavorable, embarrassing, and unacceptable situation, and one's exposure to the other, whether imaginary, real, or illusionary. Shame is not a mode that radically separates the self from the other, but in fact accomplishes the reverse. It connects the self to the other in an undesired, suffocating, and embarrassing manner. In this sense, self-awareness is not destroyed by it; instead, it is amplified. In the grip of shame, the self seeks then to escape from the world occupied by the other. However, the more desperate the attempts to escape from the unfavorable situation are, the more shameful and pained one feels deep inside. In the condition of shame, one is trapped in one's body and mind. It is the ultimate revelation of ineluctable attachment of one's body to one's mind, occurring within a personal space that is under threat of losing itself in the presence, gaze, judgment, and intimidation of the other.

The most shameful news that Uyghurs in exile have heard is perhaps the descriptions of rape inside the camps. A Uyghur survivor, Mihrigul Tursun, who was released by the CCP through the diplomatic intervention of Egypt and later came to the US, reveals how sexual violence is rampant in the camps. Abduweli Ayup, a famous Uyghur human rights activist who spent fifteen months in detention, also revealed the horror of rape he was subject to as follows:

> The first day was very bad. . . . They stripped me of my clothes, slapped my buttocks and then they abused me . . . more than 20 Chinese guys. The next day, police asked me, "One day, if you guys are in power, what will you do to us?" I said, "Look, I'm a human being, I'm not an animal like you. . . ." They want to delete Uyghur. They want Uyghurs to believe the Chinese Communist Party is God.[5]

The rape of men and women is prevalent inside China's jails and camps, a widespread sexual violation used as a heinous weapon to destroy the dignity of prisoners and inmates. It reduces them to a bodily object, upon which any type of humiliation can be indelibly inscribed.

Systematic rape as a weapon of war is described by Kozaric-Kovacic and others in the *American Journal of Orthopsychiatry* as follows:

> In the context of ethnic cleansing and genocide, the trauma of rape may be intentionally maximized by the perpetrator(s) to cause damage or death and to send a message. Physical abuse or torture, repeated assaults or gang rapes over a period of days or weeks, forced pregnancy and childbirth, the combination of

rape with the murder or torture of the survivor's loved ones, public humiliation of the survivor and her family, and verbal abuse of the survivor and her community contribute to the devastation.[6]

The latest reports, which are yet to be confirmed, have alleged that rape is being utilized systematically for reasons that are more practical, although equally abhorrent. Women are purportedly being raped with the intention of impregnating them. The women's babies are taken away when born, and the women are then forced to express their breast milk for sale to Han Chinese. Another reason for organized rape is the use of women and children for sex trafficking, inviting people into the camps and exporting women and children out for such purposes.[7]

Uyghur culture is largely conservative, and so it is extremely difficult to absorb the fact that almost all Uyghur women and girls in the camps are subject to rape. Our culture has historically cultivated a great respect for women, seeing them as the promise of a future, a bedrock of compassion, and a nurturer of community life. In the social division of labor, the man's duty is to bring bread to the table, promote the well-being of family members, and protect their safety. Women are viewed as having equal rights with men. Indeed, Uyghur businesswoman and political activist praised as Mother of Uyghurs, Rebiya Kadeer, who once served as President of the World Uyghur Congress, is a great example of this.

However, all these cultural values are now being violated and destroyed. The millions of Uyghur men interned in the camps are no longer able to provide protection for their female relatives, their mothers, sisters, wives, and daughters. Indeed, they cannot even protect themselves. Because of being unable to carry out their duty to protect Uyghur women, they feel ashamed. Uyghurs, who historically rose against the Manchus and others because of their public disrespect for Uyghur women, are now forced to accept the fact that rape is a normalized experience in the current Uyghur reality.

A Uyghur detainee, a fifty-four-year-old Kazakhstan national who was released in September 2018 from a camp in Urumqi after being detained for fifteen months, reported to *The Epoch Times* that "Young girls are taken out and raped all night long. If you keep resisting, they will inject you with something and kill you." She added that some women were given pills to stop them from becoming pregnant. She went on to reveal that she personally witnessed two Uyghur females being killed by injection, and others who were killed in different ways: "There are usually 40 to 50 people in one small room, but 5 to 10 are regularly taken out and they just disappear, they never come back. People are being killed in tens all the time."[8]

While most Uyghur men are incarcerated in camps, Han Chinese have targeted women outside the camps for forced marriage. Intermarriage has been encouraged by the CCP with financial incentives.[9] The objectives of this intermarriage are manifold. The most important objective is to assimilate Uyghur women into mainstream Chinese culture to help resolve the gender imbalance created by the one-child policy. This policy saw most Han Chinese choosing to have a boy rather than a girl. This phenomenon was widespread because Chinese families preferred a son to a daughter to prolong the paternal surname in the next generation, largely due to the importance of ancestry worship in China. The gender imbalance has complicated the prospects of Chinese men who are looking for a woman to marry. Now, there are photos published on social media and in Chinese newspapers to promote the benefits of interracial marriage between Han Chinese men and Uyghur women, and such unions are promoted as a happy event. The luxurious wedding parties are publicized to encourage more Han Chinese men to indulge in this variety of inter-ethnic marriage.

For Uyghurs in exile, these displays are hardly a reason to celebrate. On the contrary, the experience is most humiliating, as it is a state-sanctioned marriage between a perpetrator and a victim. It reveals how powerless Uyghurs are to stop this forced romance, in the end. Uyghurs can perceive this whole experience as a collective rape, all of them feeling subject to it in one way or another, inside and outside of the camps. It is the rape of Uyghurness daily, in which we feel the vicarious trauma of this horrific practice. This systematic, legalized, condoned rape is indescribably traumatic for the victims, psychologically reduced to nothing but a despicable object, or less than an object, in the process. If the victim resists, they are punished, either by being sent to the camps in even worse condition or by death. While they may try to escape from their body in the moment of sexual violence, they inevitably must be reunited with it to go on feeling the permanent and unspeakable humiliation that follows. Furthermore, they have no legal means to seek justice, as their legal rights are already denied. They have nobody—no institution and no law to protect them.

The practice of systematic rape aims to pierce the heart of Uyghur dignity. Han Chinese intend to speak to Uyghurs in a language that forces them to accept the utter destruction of their body, a collective body, which has been mutilated and now resembles a corpse. It is a cruel way to reaffirm that Han Chinese are the masters, the gentlemen from the Middle Kingdom whose ancestors have been waiting for this day. It is a most brutal way to show them they deserve this kind of animal treatment because they are subordinate humans or barbarians. The sexual satisfaction obtained through violent rape numbs them to any feelings of remorse. Instead, it enforces their ego, as they affirm themselves the dominant master of their victims, taking control of reality, fantasy, and history. It also enables them to be free from the conception of themselves as sexually inferior to barbarian Uyghurs. To rape a Uyghur woman is to reaffirm that they are sexually competent to defeat the barbarians, while also destroying the dignity of Uyghurs who are powerless to stop it. This experience has deprived Uyghurs of their dignity, humanness, and above all, their sanity . . . ultimately, everything.

All this makes us as Uyghur men feel unspeakably ashamed. We face a deep dilemma, whether to tell the world about the rape, not only the physical rape inside the camps, but also the spiritual one. We all feel this torment together in unity, beyond space and time, sharing the vicarious trauma we are going through. And yet, we are afraid to be questioned by others as to what we have done to avoid it. We have no answer for this question. Some Uyghurs even say they feel too ashamed and embarrassed to detail what is happening to the women in the camps, due to their powerlessness to stop it, which casts a shadow over their self-perceptions of masculinity. Ultimately, it questions their entire shame-ridden existence: what are you doing to prevent or stop it while being alive?

GUILT

Some of us are further overwhelmed with a sense of guilt, as an extension or result of our shame. The modality of guilt is one of the key existentialist concepts. It is, first and foremost, a psychological burden, the unpleasant and disturbing recollection of something we failed to grasp deep inside. It is the realization of responsibility for an action we feel is not right, and knowing it resides in the past, where it is irreparable. The guilt of Uyghurs is far more psychological than ontological, a survivor's guilt that some in exile are unable to rid themselves of or forget.

Rian Thum described the survival guilt among some Uyghurs as follows: "Some reach out to tell me about their family members in the concentration camps. Others ask for advice on dealing with survivor's guilt."[10] Darren Byler described this feeling in the following way: "The guilt of having escaped and survived is sometimes overwhelming. Many Uyghurs that I have become close to over the years have told me that survivor's guilt invades their dreams and takes away the small joys in their lives."[11]

Guilt is not only the acknowledgment of one's own incapacity to rectify what went wrong previously, but it is also alienation between the subject and its past, between its collective identity and its shameful reality. Ultimately, it is an acknowledgment that one is always open to the judgment of the other, irrespective of whether this other has the right, capacity, or experience to pass judgment on them, even if the other is an internalized other or an illusionary one.

In the case of Uyghurs within the camps, the pervasive sense of guilt is also a marker of their frustration with their own past, one defined by a series of painful and problematic events. The combination of these wrongdoings eventually constituted their current fate. It is a tragic fate, or kismet, that has resulted from a long series of unchangeable events, leading to their current situation in the camps.

HELPLESSNESS

Uyghurs experience the modality of helplessness in exile in the form of silent lamentation, self-loathing, and even self-condemnation. It is the internalization of one's own failures, as well as all the failures of past and current generations combined. Like guilt, it is the implicit recognition and acceptance of the impossibility and incapacity to rectify past mistakes. There is nothing left but the perception that the present and future are as condemned as the past; this genocide will continue regardless of any efforts to stop it. Further, it is the realization that our people trapped back home are not receiving help from others and are unfortunately perceived as not helpable. Within this helplessness, there is a feeling that the damage done to us by the CCP is so thorough that nobody can bring back what has been destroyed irreparably. In this sense, it is a way to resign oneself to one's own destruction, and to the destruction of one's people. Ultimately, it is a way of embracing one's own demise as a love of one's fate, as Nietzsche would say: *amor fati*.

Helplessness also results from the overwhelming feeling of being abandoned by the world. The sense of abandonment comprises varied, conflicting feelings. While we are recognized—but not assisted—as victims of the CCP's atrocities by the West, we feel especially abandoned as Muslims by the East, notably by Muslim governments. This perception is common among Uyghurs, who feel the impetus for the massacre by the CCP, in the name of re-education, is in line with the reason for their abandonment by the world—all because they are Muslims.

I had a group session in Istanbul last year for a group of Uyghurs on how to live with the collective trauma caused by genocide. Before starting my session, I asked the participants to summarize their current feelings with one word, no matter how insufficient that word was in doing justice to their myriad, complex feelings. One student told me that he feels helpless. I asked him why he feels that way. He looked deep in my eyes and sadly replied that he feels helpless even to explain to me why he feels helpless. To feel helpless, for him, is liberation from the pain and humiliation of looking into the eyes of the other for help. This liberation can make the oppressed, in the depth of helplessness, more fearless to face their situation with a strange sense of self-confidence, without seeking any external intervention. They perceive this as the last of their human dignity and are ready to face any calamity, preferring it to the humiliation of begging others, appealing to their humanity, only to be rejected or ignored. This rejection is worse for them than showing their own humiliating fear in the face of death, which might result in the loss of their faith in humanity.

In this sense, the minds of Uyghurs operate in the triangle of trauma. They consider themselves as victims who run towards the world, their rescuer, and who run from the CCP, the perpetrator. In crashing into the silent wall of the world, some Uyghurs feel abandoned and even betrayed. Some, more desperately, have been contemplating the possibility of going to the perpetrator to seek their own destruction in the same way that Uyghurs back home are destroyed.

Many other Uyghurs have expressed to me that it would be better for them to die in the camps than wait for the rescue mission from the world that will likely never come. These drastic responses may seem incomprehensible; however, when we look at the level of frustration and betrayal, we understand how some may choose death over the false hope they have long harbored, which has led to hopelessness and despair. It is, indeed, a heartbreaking last act to embrace the authenticity of human existence in a world full of false promises that beget false hope. It is a conscious liberation from an endless, deeply traumatic pain coupled with a longing to be saved. After realizing that their attempts to escape their pain and suffering by reaching out to the world—which is itself helpless in many ways—have failed, they are left only with their unending pain. With no escape left for them in this world, they are tempted to seek their escape outside this world. Death becomes their only escape from the pain after all other options are exhausted.

When one realizes the only remaining hope is to accept hopelessness, it is an act of abandoning one's ultimate dependence on the other. It is a final moment of saying farewell to humanity, so as not to embarrass it, perhaps, and making the dignified choice to face one's enemy, instead of pleading with the equally helpless humanity—being nothing but bystanders, with or without the bystander guilt.

Oddly, Uyghurs may suddenly feel, in conscious liberation, like a hero. This is odd, given that others may ridicule them for choosing immediate death over unending suffering and abandoning the fight against the atrocities of the CCP. Suicide is seen as a cowardly act, giving up seeking justice for our own people who have suffered so severely, for so long. They may still hear the call of death in their depressive mood, after no one comes to their aid. They believe death will bring back their denied dignity, on all fronts. It gives a sense of solidarity with their dying people, who are incredibly resilient in the dark black hole of the camps.

It is also a sad acknowledgment and acceptance that death for Uyghurs at the hands of the CCP is inescapable. To choose one's own death only reinforces this kismet, however dignified this death may sound. It may appear as a final conscious decision or "freedom" to choose to die rather than to be killed against your will. With no indication that we will be treated as a human anywhere in the world, what is the point of continuing to live?

In the end, all four modalities of Uyghur existence are manifestations of their philosophical, psychological, and political conditions. They paint a picture of how deeply wounded Uyghurs' souls are and how they struggle to make sense of what is happening to them. They grasp the depth and severity of their condition succinctly. Through these modalities, we can see what genocide does to a people. It not only destroys them physically, but also destroys their self-confidence and belief that they can function as a human, being part of human society. It deprives them of any assurance that they deserve a life that is equally as sacred as the life of others. They have no choice but to accept that there is no further meaning in their life as there is nothing noble, positive, or humane remaining. They believe that they are a condemned people. In the depth of their helpless condition, they are forced to face a barren future as bleak as their past.

NOTES

1. Friedrich Nietzsche, *Human, All Too Human: A Book for a Free Spirit,* Part II, New York: The MacMillan Company, 1913, 213.

2. Lin Yutang, *My Country and My People* (London: William Heineman LTD, 1936), 24–25.

3. BBC, "China Uighurs: Xinjiang Ban on Long Beards and Veils," BBC News, April 1, 2017, https://www.bbc.com/news/world-asia-china-39460538.

4. Gail Fine, *The Oxford Handbook of Plato* (Oxford, Oxford University Press, Second Edition, 2019), 191.

5. Steve Chao, "Exposed: China's Surveillance of Muslim Uighurs," Turkistantimes, Aljazeera, Feb 1, 2019, http://turkistantimes.com/en/news-10066.html.

6. Dragica Kozaric'-Kovac˘ic', Vera Folnegovic'-S˘malc, and Jarmila S˘krinjaric', "Systematic Raping of Women in Croatia and Bosnia and Herzegovina: A Preliminary Psychiatric Report," *Croatian Medical Journal 34* (1995): 87–88; Also, Dragica Kozaric'-Kovac˘ic', Vera Folnegovic'-S˘malc, Jarmila S˘krinjaric', Nathan M. Szajnberg, and Ana Marusic', "Rape, Torture and Traumatization of Bosnian and Croatian Women: Psychological Sequelae," *American Journal of Orthopsychiatry* 65 (1995): 428–33.

7. Dr. Erkin Sidiq, "Latest Information about Uyghurs in East Turkestan," Uighur Times, July 6, 2019, https://uighurtimes.com/index.php/latest-information-about-uyghurs-in-east-turkestan/.

8. Isabel Van Brugen, "Former Uyghur Inmates Tell of Torture and Rape in China's 'Re-Education' Camps," The Epoch Times, October 15, 2018, https://www.theepochtimes.com/former-uyghur-inmates-tell-of-torture-and-rape-in-chinas-re-education-camps_2689053.html.

9. Radio Free Asia, "Xinjiang Authorities Push Uyghurs to Marry Han Chinese," Radio Free Asia, 2017, https://www.rfa.org/english/news/special/uyghur-oppression/ChenPolicy2.html.

10. Rian Thum, "How an American TV Show Captured the Extent of Chinese Repression," *Washington Post*, May 9, 2019, https://www.washingtonpost.com/opinions/2019/05/09/how-an-american-tv-show-captured-extent-chinese-repression/?noredirect=on&utm_term=.f67fc58653fc.

11. Darren Byler, "'The Night Is Thick': Uyghur Poets Respond to the Disappearance of Their Relatives," SupChina, March 6, 2019, https://supchina.com/2019/03/06/uyghur-poets-respond-to-the-disappearance-of-their-relatives/.

Chapter Four

The Creation of a Culture of Killing

It is forbidden to kill; therefore, all murderers are punished unless they kill in large numbers and to the sound of trumpets.

—Voltaire

PHILOSOPHICAL INTELLECTUALS' PERCEPTION OF GENOCIDE

Let me start with the philosophical thoughts of Emmanuel Levinas. As a Holocaust survivor, he makes a radical philosophical shift in search of the meaning of "being the other" within the context of ethical thinking after the Second World War. He does not explicitly reflect on the Holocaust in his philosophical works; however, his works are a relevant reference to fundamental lessons of genocide against Jews. To understand broader implications and move beyond the Holocaust, Levinas does not simply blame Hitler, or Germans who followed the ideals and orders of Hitler, the Third Reich, or German culture. Instead, he focuses on how the philosophical tradition of the West, the Western way of thinking, led to the destruction of millions of innocent lives through its inevitable intellectual habit of totalization.

At its heart, the Levinasian philosophy wrestles with how we understand the incomprehensible (the other or the alterity) from within the comprehensible (the self). Levinas criticizes the Western philosophical tradition for ultimately placing the other within the sphere of the self, reducing it to concepts and ideas within the self, in a process that he calls totalization. He asserts this as a form of violence against the other as prevalent in Western philosophical thinking. He traces the origins of this totalizing tendency through the veins of philosophy to rationalize it, attempting to render the incomprehensible comprehensible.

For Levinas, philosophy is the highest form of rationality. Therefore, if the origin of the genocide against the Jewish people as "the other" during WWII is ultimately philosophical, then it is possible to understand it rationally. This attempt by Levinas to rationalize the Holocaust puts him in contention with the position of some other Holocaust survivors, who insist that it is impossible to speak the unspeakable, to apportion a rationale to the irrational. Yet, his rare insight into the anatomy of Western thought and its role in reducing the other to the self leads him to conclude that the Holocaust is a deeply philosophical matter, even if he fails to acknowledge the other constitutive elements of this genocide, which remain largely irrational and unreasonable.

Levinas asserts in his reflection on forgiveness, "One can forgive many Germans, but there are some Germans it is difficult to forgive. It is difficult to forgive Heidegger."[1] As we examine Levinas's position, comparing Martin Heidegger's philosophical ideologies to a flirtation with Nazism, it is understandable he considers Heidegger unforgivable.

As one of the most prominent philosophers of the twentieth century, one who was thinking through both rationalism and idealism prior to the Holocaust, Heidegger should have understood the evil aspects of genocide better than anybody else. Perhaps this is why it is difficult for Levinas to accept the unforgivable mistakes of Heidegger, who is idealized by some as an epitome of humanity, a perfect human being, in whom both rationality and passion are perfectly combined. As ancient Greek philosophers proposed, he appeared to live in the world of ideas or *nous*, including the Platonic ideas of Good, Truth, and Justice. However, Heidegger was also a normal and finite human being, prone to making mistakes, not necessarily of ignorance, but of misjudgment, selfishness, and shortsightedness. This is one of the fundamental modes of Being-in-the-world, which Heidegger may or may not accept.

Heidegger's controversial philosophical positions prior to and during the genocide illustrate that not everyone in Germany during WWII was immune to the temptations, seductions, and, ultimately, brainwashing of the Nazi ideology. Certainly, Heidegger's sympathy toward Nazism was perplexing, given Hitler's argument of exterminating Jewish people, not normally acceptable in any ethical thinking or system. However, he evidently found the ideology rationalistic enough to be convincing, despite it being contradictory to his own fundamental philosophical treatise.

At the highest level of philosophy, critical thinking is paramount. Heidegger somehow failed to evaluate critically the concept of Nazism, despite his extraordinary intellectual capacity and opportunity to do so. Further, it is critical to note that some continue to glorify him as one of the great German philosophers, despite his ambiguous ethical position during the Nazi regime. This position is deeply disturbing—it is not a position of a person who is gullible or simple-minded, unable to discern good from evil. It is the position of a great philosopher who knows all western ethical theories intimately and who has formulated unique ethical theories of his own. This shows us that neither our ethical thinking nor our knowledge of the world and human condition can save us from the influence of the heinous ideologies of genocide. Heidegger's ethical inconsistency demonstrates that Nazism is a dangerous ideology with the potential to nullify the critical thinking capacity of anyone, regardless of profession, ethnicity, or previous ethical predisposition. As we move on from the legacy of Heidegger and others, we will continue to see this fascination and rationalization of genocidal ideologies, despite their obvious flaws.

THE RESPONSIBILITY OF CHINESE INTELLECTUALS

Sympathy for genocide pervades our personal, cultural, and political thought paradigms. Our minds often process it, not in the realm of reason, but within the survivalist, fight-or-flight mentality of the unconscious. This primitive mentality overrides our rational critical-thinking capacity. The irrational but powerful belief that your life depends on your aggressive drive to obliterate an enemy can provide a false sense of satisfaction and safety. As such, the acceptance of prejudicial and unrealistic perceptions of an enemy will justify aggression, bringing it to the surface and consequentially enacted.

In addition, within cultural and political paradigms, being sympathetic to genocide is a byproduct of belonging to an elitist political culture. This culture shapes the way we, as a collective people, think, act, react, and reflect. To be defined, captivated by, and accepted into this culture is palpably dangerous. The demonization of a selected group in this cultural landscape can make genocide seem a fascinating idea, a convincing argument, a political necessity, or sacred duty, so overwhelmingly making it a rational solution to historical political impasses. Like thick fog, it engulfs every aspect of our thinking, making our surroundings hazy and blurry, providing an illusion that our heinous actions are absolutely right and historically justifiable.

Within this context, the question arises, which Chinese intellectuals should I select for my forgiveness, given their role of silence, complicity or indeed propagation of the genocide of Uyghurs? I acknowledge that, gradually, some Chinese dissidents in exile have finally broken their silence and expressed their disagreement with genocidal policies of the CCP towards Uyghurs, Kazakhs, and others in East Turkistan. For example, on August 10, 2018, approximately 47 Chinese intellectuals and others in exile issued an appeal against what they described as "shocking human rights atrocities perpetrated in Xinjiang."[2] Yet, many others have remained utterly silent over the crisis, even though it unfolds before their very eyes, or at least within the scope of their awareness through the global media. I am apprehensive, not about the ones who express sympathy towards the ongoing crisis, but about the many others who seem indifferent to the cruelty of the CCP. I am, therefore, interested in exploring the inner psychological mechanism behind the pervasive indifference of the majority of Han Chinese and, more specifically, Han Chinese intellectuals to the Uyghur genocide.

Among Chinese intellectuals, the most powerful reflection on the Uyghur issue comes, indirectly, from leading Chinese intellectual Wang Lixiong, in his book called *My Western Regions, Your East Turkistan* (我的西域,你的东突). Wang Lixiong analyzes the political reality of Tibetans and Uyghurs at a deeper level. In his book, he describes the attitude of Chinese intellectuals to Uyghurs as follows:

> However, I am more shocked by Han intellectuals, including some elites at the top. On any normal day, they appear to be open-minded, reasonable, and supportive of reform, but as soon as we touch the topic of Xinjiang, the word 'kill' streams out of their mouths with such facility. If genocide can keep Xinjiang under China's sovereignty, I think it is possible that they will be able to stay composed and quiet if millions of Uighurs are killed. [3]

This book was written back in 2007, not a recent publication. Since then, the Uyghur genocide has continued to escalate unabated. It remains unclear what has made these intellectuals so hateful towards Uyghurs. However, it is not difficult to imagine that Chinese intellectuals were already covertly justifying and intellectually rationalizing this genocide for more than a decade prior to its inception. The organized mental preparation of these intellectuals for the Uyghur genocide coincided with the preliminary intent and actual execution undertaken by the CCP. Indeed, it is clear that this genocide has always enjoyed wide public support among Han intellectuals. The question, then, is why has the CCP postponed the execution of this genocide? The CCP has delayed their actions, quite deliberately and calculatedly, ensuring the cementation of support through the propaganda and brainwashing of Han Chinese, to the point where they were ready to accept, defend, and execute the genocide without question.

The CCP created genocidal ideation within the minds of some intellectuals, who then propagated it further within the minds of the masses. It is now being carried out under the sweeping order of the CCP, an almost unstoppable juggernaut that combines the collective effort of the media, government agencies, and officials. The difference between these intellectuals and the CCP is this: intellectuals have the hidden desire to kill Uyghurs, but their role in the genocide is as a communicative weapon of the CCP, and they have no concept or knowledge of the practicable execution of it. The CCP, however, is the primary actor, conducting the genocide of Uyghurs covertly and silently behind high barbed-wire walls.

It is difficult to fathom what motivates Chinese intellectuals to promote the indiscriminate killing of Uyghurs. I offer the following suggestions. Perhaps they seek the elimination of potential "Uyghur terrorists" from their society; or perhaps, it is an expression of the hatred buried in their collective unconsciousness against "barbarians," a label historically defining Uyghurs. It could be that they are attempting to exclude them from the ultimate unification of the Chinese nation (中华民族), into which Uyghurs have refused to be assimilated. They may be economically motivated, enthusiastic to realize the Chinese Dream (中国梦) of their emerging nation-state, turned into a Chinese nightmare for Uyghurs who seek freedom. All or any of these options are possible. However, what is still deeply incomprehensible to me is how any of these reasons could seem valid in justifying the propagation of the Uyghur genocide.

The CCP has used cognitive pre-conditioning to ingrain this instant categorization in the psyche of Han Chinese, who will not be punished for expressing their hatred towards Uyghurs in any way; on the contrary, it is encouraged and rewarded, if only tacitly. However, if Uyghur intellectuals use this same expression, the rule is completely reversed. Expressing support for killing Uyghurs is quite a natural and admirable thing for Chinese intellectuals to do; however, for a Uyghur intellectual to speak of killing, or even any ill will towards Han Chinese, is a cardinal sin, used as justification for their incarceration in concentration camps or for labeling them as either terrorists, separatists, or both. These twisted rules of linguistic expression are internalized and, hence, normalized in the Han Chinese psyche. It remains challenging to rationalize these dangerous, instinctual desires of Chinese intellectuals to kill Uyghurs effectively.

I firmly believe these Chinese intellectuals must have had memories of the great famine in China from 1959 to 1961, which claimed the lives of millions of Han Chinese and other ethnic minorities as one of the worst man-made catastrophes in history, for which the CCP is responsible. In addition, these Chinese intellectuals must have had memories of the massacre carried out by Red Guards against any dissident intellectuals during the Cultural Revolution and, finally, the Tiananmen Square massacre. All these disasters killed Han Chinese and others indiscriminately, and some of them even targeted a great number of intellectuals. After reflecting on these memories, I am bewildered and find it difficult to understand how these same intellectuals remain so unquestioningly loyal to the CCP. This is the same CCP who has killed Chinese intellectuals before, and to a lesser extent (probably due to a decline in numbers, and hence opportunity) is still doing so, just as it is committing genocide against Uyghurs.

In this context, the only explanation for their attitude and behavior that I can offer is the psychological theory of Stockholm syndrome. This mental state develops when a victim of a hostage-taking or kidnapping develops feelings of trust, affection, and dependency for the perpetrator, their captor. In this syndrome, when the captor who has power over them chooses not to kill them, victims consider it an act of kindness and benevolence. With the terrifying threat of death lifted, they are granted life—however temporarily—and the survivor experiences a huge sense of relief, rejuvenation, and even bliss. This psychological transformation, however delusional, can mean that victims are so grateful for the life-giving choice of their captor, as if they have witnessed the divine moment of creation. In the moment they realize they will not be killed, they are seized with a deep sense of gratitude to the perpetrator who spared them in this act of kindness. Unfortunately, the trauma of being threatened with and then saved from death alters their psyche so substantially that they are no longer able to feel any sympathy or empathy towards others who are imprisoned, tortured, or even killed by the same captors.

Of course, not all victims of violence or life-threatening events respond by developing Stockholm syndrome. It begins to develop when victims lose the ability to recognize their perpetrators as a perpetrator. This delusional and unquestioningly loyal gratitude towards the perpetrator develops during captivity as a defense mechanism against the ever-present threat of death, and it becomes their reality. Each time the perpetrator threatens and then saves them reinforces their delusion.

In some cases, this conditioning is so powerful that the delusion continues long after the captivity has ended. Despite their reality changing and the threat of death being removed, it may not bring about a radical change in their physical roles and circumstances within their society. The victim, psychologically speaking, has the same psychic disposition, character, and personality before, during, and after the capture. Critically, these changes only occur in their psyche, but not in their physical or conscious reality. However, their psyche misconstrues the nature of their reality because of their distorted perceptions and delusions. Importantly, it is also the perpetrator calculatedly implanting, distorting, and reinforcing this delusional psyche within their victims, in this case, the CCP perpetrated on their Han Chinese victims.

For Chinese intellectuals, things are slightly different. While they may be categorized as victims of Stockholm syndrome, their predilection for and even obsession with killing Uyghurs creates another level of complexity. In Stockholm syndrome, a victim does not lose the original role of victimhood, but their perception of the perpetrator changes into a benevolent savior in their delusional alternate reality. Crucially, despite this perceived role-change, the victim still recognizes they are the victim, even as they are no longer opposed to the perpetrator.

The Chinese intellectuals, on the other hand, feel compelled further to align their ideological framework, their paradigms, and their behaviors with the CCP, creating a sense of identification and belonging. It has become natural for them to think and act in compliance with the CCP, bringing to fruition the decade-long thought reforms and self-censorship. The result is the manifestation of genocide against Uyghurs, as their "benevolent savior" commands. They have lost the cognitive capacity to differentiate between victim and perpetrator, as they are both a victim in reality and a perpetrator in illusion. This deluded self-perception prevents them from keeping a critical distance from what is as dangerous for them as it is for Uyghurs, the CCP. Through their actions, they become simply a dangerous extension of the CCP or a useful tool it leverages to exert influence in Chinese society. In the event they cease to be useful or become detrimental, the CCP will not hesitate to dispose of them as well, despite their loyalty.

This phenomenon can be called Beijing syndrome, which is different from Stockholm syndrome. The former describes a psychological state wherein the victim acts as a self-appointed or volunteer perpetrator, while still occasionally defining themselves as victims, where necessary. Feeling the pressing need for self-preservation, the victim escalates to greater levels of violence to demonstrate to the perpetrator that they are not a victim, the passive receiver of violence, but a perpetrator as well, though the impact is temporary and conditional. They must repeatedly prove their capacity to inflict the same or worse violence upon their victims, becoming an active perpetrator themselves. This is a strange way to cope with the enormous psychological burden of being a victim, to turn oneself into a perpetrator, compensating for the pain, suffering, and humiliation of victimhood. Their life is given meaning, in their fantasy world, through the projection of violence upon the weak, defenseless, and hated. This power over others, then, feeds their ego, promoting them from victimhood to the status of perpetrator. In so doing, they will survive and rise from the depths of their suffering, idolizing the authority and power of their own perpetrators and hoping, perhaps, that they themselves will be idolized in the same way.

For some, Beijing syndrome may be a manifestation of their unconscious insecurity, a profound fear of being a victim with no legal security to speak truth to or challenge their higher authority, the CCP. If so, they would likely repudiate the existence of this syndrome, reducing it to a petty political reaction of a Uyghur intellectual, perhaps even born out of envy of the status of the Chinese intellectuals. However, the widespread manifestations of this phenomenon suggest that there are far more disturbing factors at play that require further examination.

The Cultural Revolution's purgation of "untrustworthy" intellectuals inside the CCP brought political and personal havoc for Chinese intellectuals. Deeply traumatized, they thoroughly internalized their grief over the loss and impact on their spirituality and humanity. Abstract literature reveals the impact only to a certain extent, as it was subject to censorship by the CCP. The wounds of the collective trauma, properly called "scar literature" or literature of the wounded (伤痕文学), represented the suffering of a whole generation who experienced subjugation, purgation, and elimination.

This trauma was eventually addressed by the CCP, but the responsibility was placed only on the historical mistakes of the Four Gangs, and not on the CCP as a whole. The transference of responsibility for the political chaos to a small clique of "revisionists" saved the face of the CCP. Examined critically, however, the Cultural Revolution exposed the danger posed by the CCP. Under the guise of democratic reflections on past mistakes, they revealed how the natural tendency of totalitarianism, while it seeks to maintain political power, is a consolidation of abusive control in the hands of a few party elites. Above all, it laid bare the danger of the fanatical idolization of the leader at the time, Mao Zedong. He was praised as an eternal savior of the people, all while masterminding their mass killings through famine, political infighting, and purges.

The greatest irony of the Chinese totalitarian regime is that while the CCP is continuously praised as a great savior of Han Chinese from adversity, evil, and extinction, it has been and remains the greatest mastermind and executioner of such crimes, up to and including genocide. Here, the Chinese version of *maodun* (矛盾), the Chinese word for contradiction, is relevant in that a horrific murderer is at the same time a compassionate protector. Historically, most of the communist Chinese leaders have always had two faces: they are a murderer and a savior at once, the combination of which within a single person or institution is almost too complex to comprehend.

However, it would be remiss of me not to note that the CCP has great experience in managing public perception and skillfully reconciles this contradiction, not through the power of intellectualism but through pervasive intimidation. Fear is instilled so deeply within the Chinese heart that it finds it difficult to differentiate the murderer from the savior. In each heart, the two faces are reconciled, or dialectically synthesized, in such a way that it seems natural that the murderer could also protect the people by destroying the life and culture of the appointed enemy. Stated inversely, the protector kills an (imaginary) enemy, protecting people from its destruction. In extreme cases, this murder is conducted in the name of protecting people from themselves.

The common essential ingredient of this ideology and survivalist mentality is the creation of an enemy. Previously, it was the petty bourgeois revisionists, Westernized intellectuals, landowners, and others, who were singled out and then suppressed as enemies of the state during the Cultural Revolution. Now, the CCP is turning to Uyghurs, propagating their reputation as the enemy of the state, a fatal threat to the security of Chinese society and, politically speaking, to the Chinese Dream. The way that the CCP has turned the entire Uyghur population into an enemy from within is similarly two-faced and much more extreme, or bipolar, than what Uyghur intellectuals are accused of. The CCP can destroy Uyghurs through genocide, while simultaneously acting as a savior, saving Uyghurs—by killing them, if necessary—from the pitfalls of terrorism.

The CCP used the same logic and methodology in the Cultural Revolution (Han Chinese as victims) as they now do in the Uyghur genocide (Han Chinese promoted to perpetrators). The threat is to be completely contained or eliminated in a place where it can be carried out secretly and efficiently through ideological quarantine. Those who fail to pass the requirements of quarantining must be killed without mercy to protect the vital interests of Han Chinese, for to kill is to protect. The difference between these two scenarios is that the former was, for the most part, a targeted approach to eliminate certain individuals with some collateral damage, whereas the latter features the indiscriminate confinement and killings of men, women, and children because all Uyghurs are now the enemy. The killing, however much it has intensified, is justified without difficulty. It is justified because the CCP has refined a series of political tactics, not only to create an enemy from within, but also to eliminate it, all with the acquiescence of the fully desensitized Han Chinese. As such, they have been indoctrinated not to question this violence on any level, for to do so is to be seen as weak-hearted and feeble-minded by the enemy and, ultimately, by the CCP and could lead to becoming victims themselves.

The CCP cleverly uses other methods to justify killing innocent people in the name of protecting the people's interests. In particular, the CCP can mobilize state-controlled mass media across the country within a short timeframe, with astonishing effectiveness. The CCP has demonstrated an effective yet simple mastery in running these campaigns, appealing to the foundational instincts of Han Chinese through carefully crafted language.

LANGUAGE AS A DECEPTIVE POLITICAL TOOL

Language in the political arena of China is an integral part of the propaganda that allows for dissemination of the agenda of the CCP. When used adeptly, it redefines reality within such an illusion that truth unfolds in language, and not the other way around. It creates a parallel world, which it applies thoroughly and misleadingly to the real world. This parallel world mirrors and overshadows the real world, making it invisible, inaudible, and indistinguishable, until ultimately the real world becomes blurred and unrecognizable. All that is seen, acknowledged, and lived in is the parallel world that is carefully and deliberately created by the CCP. This barrier between the real world and the imaginary one serves as a space where reality can be manipulated. Here, the CCP inserts political fabrications and a ruthless agenda into the minds of the people; history is edited and adjusted, and enemies are both created and eliminated as required by the CCP.

The famous Chinese thinker, Lin Yutang, notices the inter-connectedness in China between language and politics. For him, the former is an essential foundation and even the heart of the latter, as follows:

> For the Chinese have developed an art of mincing words—largely due, as we have seen, to the monosyllabic character of the literary language—and we believe in words. It is words by which we live and words which determine the victory in a political or legal struggle. . . . The party that finds a better-sounding pretext wins in the eyes of the public. The dead language therefore became a dishonest language. Anything is permissible as long as you call it by the wrong name.[4]

No other politically defined terms in China have more negative connotations and provoke such emotional disgust than these three: "维吾尔族" (Uyghurs), "疆独" (Xinjiang independence), and "恐怖分子" (terrorists). The CCP uses these three terms interchangeably, as the words are skillfully synonymized with a campaign of genius propaganda. This systematic vilification of Uyghurs was accomplished by skewing the reality of the Urumqi massacre in 2009 (when Uyghurs were suppressed after attempting to seek justice for the bloody brawl in Shaoguan),[5] and later, the Tiananmen Square incident. Finally, the CCP cited the Kunming attack, which was claimed by a shadowy Uyghur terrorist gang as one of their operations inside China. The CCP has combined and distorted these incidents, using them collectively as proof that Uyghurs are terrorists, and broadcasting this conclusion as fact through state-controlled mass media. It has implanted a simple equation or explanation in the minds of Han Chinese, the belief that Uyghurs are an ethnic minority with a heinous political agenda to gain independence, intent on seceding from the motherland by means of violent terrorism.

This synonymity has three levels: psychological, linguistic, and political. On a psychological level, many Han Chinese believe that the imaginary "terroristic" behaviors of Uyghurs can only be explained as an act of ungratefulness (忘恩负义), considering the "preferential treatment" they receive from the CCP. This perception is best understood through the lens of Confucianism, a deeply ingrained influence in Han Chinese culture. Within this context, Uyghurs are seen as children who have betrayed the care of the mother (or Motherland). The promotion of loyalty (忠) is of paramount importance to the CCP. The acts of Uyghurs are represented as being disloyal, which provoke not simply anger, but, more fundamentally, hatred in Han Chinese.

After the Cultural Revolution, the CCP readopted the principal of *Ren* (仁), which "implies a paternalistic government whose duty is to look after the weak and the poor."[6] In the Confucian culture, *Ren* is a key virtue, exemplifying a parent's protective feelings and behaviors for their children. However, this concept of protection has different connotations when applied in the context of a government's relationship to the people, with real-world manifestations that are considerably less benign. The CCP holds a deeply paternalistic and patronizing attitude towards all Chinese citizens, treating them as children who require constant care provided by officials, institutions, legislation, laws, and government bureaucrats. It never allows the "children" to do things independently and denies their identity as mature adults, crippling their freedom and capacity to protect themselves.

On the other hand, this virtue expects the children (or adult Han Chinese) to show their loyalty (忠) to the parents (or the CCP) unconditionally. Furthermore, discipline and punishment are a fundamental part of this parental care; children can be disciplined and punished as harshly as possible for their behavioral problems for their own wellbeing. Chinese culture dictates an asymmetrical relation between parents and children, so parents are rarely questioned on the measures of discipline and punishment they use. The respect for parents as authoritative figures is one of the key social virtues in Chinese culture. This mainstream value has been hijacked by the CCP pretending to be the parents of all Chinese citizens as a socio-political measure to curb any potential criticism or dissent, justifying the use of whatever force they deem necessary.

Linguistically, the name Uyghur (维吾尔) literally translates into English as "you who safeguards me," meaning Uyghurs have a duty to safeguard their mother, or the motherland. As Uyghurs live in the marginal areas, historically known as Western Regions (西域), they were required to be loyal subjects, as a people protected by the kings of the Middle Kingdom. This linguistic connection is not readily apparent to many Han Chinese, but it can be used by the CCP in many subtle ways.

Uyghurs who seek political deviation from the orbit of this Middle Kingdom have been regarded as renegades who are in denial of the primordial linguistic agreement between Uyghurs and their parental protectors. This unspoken agreement is as sacred as a legal contract and cannot tolerate betrayal. If any betrayal emerges, this same language will be evoked by the CCP, calling it an unforgivable act of disloyalty as they mete out severe punishment. This language has already made it clear that the actions are criminal, even without the need for legal scrutiny, so the CCP can easily explain to ordinary Han Chinese why Uyghurs must be punished severely. For, these same linguistic terms that the CCP misuses and abuses are the very terms that Han Chinese people are already familiar with, within the context of Confucianism. In this way, the dialectical meaning of identical linguistics is delivered as one simple message from the CCP to both Han Chinese and Uyghurs. Uninterrupted communication successfully serves the interest of the CCP on both fronts.

Politically, the term "Uyghur separatism" creates a deep sense of anxiety among Han Chinese, who have been taught that Xinjiang has been an inseparable part of motherland China since antiquity. For decades, the CCP has made it a political imperative that the motherland steadfastly opposes any acts of separatism. This includes their complete opposition to Xinjiang independence, Tibet independence, Taiwan independence, and, more recently, their subtle attempts to encroach on Hong Kong's freedom movements. Separatism is unthinkable and inadmissible in the public consciousness, going to the heart of the political cosmology created by the CCP, which projects an image of China as a complete whole, unbreakable and indivisible. According to this political cosmology, which is shrouded in a political myth, separation is a movement of seceding from pre-existing political totality, order, and sacredness, inevitably leading to disintegration, disorder, and profanity.

This political myth sounds sacred, indeed. Such a vision reminds Han Chinese of the history of its warring states, conflicts, and foreign rule; but also, more deeply, it threatens their most basic sense of safety. The sense of threat is so extreme that it reinforces the CCP's role as the savior, protecting the people from this alarming possibility. In such a world, a cyclical movement of evil reins everyone in. The more dangerous the enemy becomes, the greater the need for protection of the CCP, which, in turn, increases the desperation of people, who then turn to the CCP for protection. In such a world, as long as there is an enemy, Han Chinese will immediately desire the CCP's intervention and protection. Likewise, in the event the people do not desire the CCP as a legitimate state, the CCP could be quick to create a new enemy to position itself as the savior of the people.

Within this context, exaggerated allegations the CCP has made of connections between Uyghurs and the international terrorist movement has proved fatal for Uyghurs indiscriminately. The CCP has been able to link the war on terror strongly to Uyghur discontentment by magnifying their religious faith, casting it as extremism, to a point where there is no perceived difference between peaceful religious practice and terroristic activities. The very mention of Uyghurs now fills the hearts of Han Chinese with the terror of violence, along with the betrayal of separatism, as the term terrorism (恐怖主义) in Chinese signifies.

In these ways, the combination of three concepts has linguistically painted an image of Uyghurs as untrustworthy, ungrateful, dangerous, and violent. Before the concentration camp detentions had even begun, the CCP had already defined Uyghurs linguistically and sentenced them to heavy punishment. This manifested in the treatment by Han Chinese of marginalization, humiliation, and suppression, becoming a daily experience of Uyghurs. No mercy and compassion is left for them, inherently viewed as monsters inside China and forever defamed. It is not surprising, then, that they have since been displaced and forced into concentration camps, disregarded by Han Chinese. The CCP was confident they had tarnished the image of Uyghurs sufficiently to avoid eliciting any mercy from Han Chinese. They were certain no one would come to their aid. Uyghurs were to be eliminated, and the CCP have full support of Han Chinese to do so. It is with this conviction and confidence that Xi Jinping has been emboldened to take such draconian steps, putting millions of Uyghurs in camps in front of the whole world in general and of Han Chinese in particular. He knew the reaction to his decisions would be minimal and easy to overcome, in time.

VIOLENCE NORMALIZED

It is easy to see that the CCP has been extremely successful in normalizing violence inside China. Public propaganda is one of the best methods for brainwashing people. In order to carry out violence unopposed, the CCP applies a variety of linguistic strategies to simply designate the enemy with a succinct name, phrase, or metaphor. For example, to marginalize the intellectuals during the Cultural Revolution, the CCP called them "revisionists"; to suppress the Tiananmen youth, the CCP called the intellectuals supporting them "black hands"; and to eliminate Uyghurs, they called them "terrorists." By virtue of these labels, they have tacitly demonized these groups, recreating their identity into a single, narrow, negative, stereotyped category. The acceptance of this caricature has laid the groundwork for the larger belief in a binary opposition between the safe, protective, and wise CCP and a despicable enemy.

Almost all of the CCP's linguistic strategies are designed to incorporate binary oppositions, irreconcilable in principle, in the form of dualism as key to the implantation of simple yet powerful perceptions in the minds of the masses. Predominantly, the belief is that one party must subdue the other party by force. Usually, the CCP is the dominant party whose task is to subdue the other dissenting parties. This linguistic dualism is a powerful means to attain a political goal, creating an internal enemy and justifying its ruthless suppression. The use of this dualism is a psychological tactic the CCP employs to promote an attitude of urgency, assuring that a lingering and prolonged confrontation between opposing sides will not be tolerated. As such, this sense of urgency makes the immediacy of the suppression both legitimate and expeditious.

By using an ancient thought model to simplify the complexity of the relationship between different parties, the CCP motivates the masses to find a solution to this stagnant confrontation through action. Through this tactic of dualism, the CCP successfully positions itself as a party that can surge to victory in a life-and-death conflict over the enemies it has created. In this world, the imperative of "kill-or-be-killed" dictates everything, and there is

no consideration for reconciliation in such a tense and confrontational environment. In the case of Uyghurs, the CCP has created an effective psychological distaste within the public, positioning them as the targeted enemy and
soliciting a strong desire to punish them. In most of the cases, the Chinese
masses act at best as indifferent bystanders, at worst as executioners of the
CCP's will.

Lin Yutang speaks on behalf of Chinese intellectuals, who are afraid to
act bravely following the voice of conscience. They act in the name of
pacifism, which is a cover-up word for their cowardice:

> Pacifism, too, is a matter of high human understanding. If man could learn to
> be a little more cynical, he would also be less inclined toward warfare. That is
> perhaps why all intelligent men are cowards. The Chinese are the world's
> worst fighters because they are an intelligent race, backed and nurtured by
> Taoistic cynicism and the Confucian emphasis on harmony as the ideal of life.
> They do not fight because they are the most calculating and self-interested of
> peoples. An average Chinese child knows what the European grey-haired
> statesmen do not know, that by fighting one gets killed or maimed, whether it
> be an individual or a nation. [7]

He attributes this cowardice to a lack of political security in Chinese society.
For him, intelligent men prefer non-action to action in a society where there
is no basic protection of law and order. Instead of acting, they indulge themselves in Taoist cynicism and Confucian loyalty, both of which promise them
a secure life free of the ever-present political risk of dissent against the CCP.

Let us take Uyghurs in China as an example to demonstrate the indifferent attitude of Han Chinese in general and of Chinese intellectuals in particular to others' pain and suffering. Under the rule of the CCP, Uyghurs have
learned they must be wholeheartedly loyal, or the consequences are too great.
Many Uyghurs have internalized this simple rule, becoming obedient to Han
Chinese rule for the sake of securing their life and experiencing less political
risk. This rule, this regime, and the CCP are, theoretically speaking, the same
for both Uyghurs and Han Chinese. There is, however, one fundamental
difference between Uyghurs and Han Chinese who are living under the rule
of the CCP. Han Chinese have no obligation, nor any duty to assimilate
themselves into mainstream culture. They are expected to be subordinate
citizens and not pose a threat to the interests of the CCP, but they are under
no obligation to go through cultural transformations and psychological indoctrination to accept the mainstream Chinese culture. Uyghurs, on the other
hand, are required to go through both political subordination and cultural
assimilation.

Moreover, Uyghurs must endure daily discrimination from the mainstream Han Chinese majority and treatment as a social anomaly, unfit for the
decent cultural milieu and high political echelons. Unlike ordinary Chinese,

who have cultural protection in Taoism and Confucianism and some political capital in the network of overwhelmingly Han Chinese society, Uyghurs have nothing of the sort. They are bare-faced and easily recognizable, labeled arbitrarily as dangerous terrorists on the street, with no opportunity to prove they are harmless. They walk under the constantly suspicious gaze of Han Chinese who do not trust them or see them as aliens, as expressed in the Chinese adage: "Those who are not our kind are sure to be of a different heart" (非我族类, 其心必异).

This society does not accept them as genuine compatriots but rather abandons them as complete outsiders, strangers, and aliens. As a result, Uyghurs cannot regard themselves truly as part of Chinese society. In fact, they detach themselves from it to a certain extent, for to do otherwise is to deny their ancestry, identity, spirituality, and culture, which would be impossible. In these mutually exclusive perceptions, both parties blame the other for the separation and segregation. For Uyghurs, this separation is significant as they do not want to be assimilated into Chinese society at the expense of losing their unique identity, and Han Chinese do not want to accept them genuinely as part of their society, perceiving them as barbarians. In the end, Uyghurs find themselves in an impossible situation—allowed neither to be Uyghurs nor Han Chinese. They are stuck between possibility and impossibility, between being an enemy or a *Xinjiangren* (新疆人, a Xinjiang person), a Muslim terrorist or an atheist Chinese citizen. In short, they are as much a political dilemma for themselves as for the Chinese.

In such a repressive environment, Uyghurs have taken one political risk after another to fight for their right simply to exist as a Uyghur. They are all aware of the political costs of being brave in China, but this has not deterred them. Although some might call this political temerity, they never cease claiming what rights entitle to them: to be treated as a human with a unique identity, dignified and respected. This demand is simply encapsulated in Confucianism as the golden rule: "Do not do to others what you do not want them to do to you."

Lin Yutang also talks about indifference as a key Chinese characteristic. Prior to examining his view on it, I would like to discuss a disturbing video clip that circulated in the social media recently. The video showed a young girl who was crossing at a pedestrian crosswalk somewhere in China. She was suddenly hit and driven over by a taxi, which did not stop, but drove away. There were other cars passing by and other pedestrians in the crosswalk. To my surprise, none of them stopped and came immediately to her aid. Instead, the cars drove around her while the pedestrians continued to cross the intersection to reach the other side, all without approaching her. The whole scene felt like fiction, frightening, mysterious, and surreal, as if it did not happen. It felt like the girl was not human, but a walking ghost who did not get any human support, only divine grace. The indifference of the

people, both in cars and on foot, to the injured or dying girl, was overwhelmingly shocking. One could only wonder if they had any human emotions, to
be unaffected by the suffering of another human being in such a horrific
situation. What is deeply disturbing in this scene is not only the cold-blooded
apathy of people, but also their inner composition not to be affected by
external trouble (麻烦).

Here, we should consider their attitude in the context of the notion of *Wu-
wei* or doing nothing (无为) in Taoism, defined in a paradoxical way as the
action of non-action. *Wu-wei* signifies supreme effortlessness, defining a
non-action as a form of action by following the rhythm and cycles of the
natural world. It can also be defined as the wisdom of social disengagement
(withdrawal) as opposed to social engagement—the subtle cultivation of a
state of being where actions should be as natural as breathing, without being
affected by external incidents, changes, and events, which are largely uncontrollable. Alternatively, perhaps it is the most sophisticated form of pretense
that shows no action while acting in hiding. This is a refinement of personality in a world where nothing is certain or predictable, and where overt action
draws suspicion and is considered a sign of dishonesty or showiness. Is this
the perfected personality, displaying civility while nurturing the courage not
to be disturbed by external stimulation, problems, and troubles? Is this the
description of some Han Chinese, who behave as bystanders, not actors on
the social stage? If this is the intrinsic attitude of some Han Chinese, then it is
not hard to imagine them turning a blind eye to what is happening unjustly,
not only to their own people, but also, quite naturally, to Uyghurs. Their
welfare is subject to even greater apathy than that of any other Han Chinese,
in terms of social protection and racial biases. In the end, Uyghurs' pain and
suffering are consumed by the cold, calculated, and pitiless apathy of Han
Chinese.

On the subject of indifference as one of the Chinese characteristics, Lin
Yutang writes as follows:

> I think this indifference is not a natural characteristic of the people, but is a
> conscious product of our culture, deliberately inculcated by our old-world
> wisdom under the special circumstances. . . . In other words, indifference has a
> distinct "survival value" in China. . . . The "survival-value" of indifference
> consists, therefore, in the fact that in the absence of protection of personal
> rights, it is highly unsafe for a man to take too much interest in public affairs,
> or "idle affairs," as we call them. [8]

Again, the view of Lin Yutang can be contested based on the simple fact that
both Uyghurs and Han Chinese are living under the same political system.
There is a stark contrast between the different perspectives and responses of
these two groups, however, when it comes to being indifferent to political
matters. Strictly speaking, both live under the same rule of survival. Yet,

Uyghurs are fighting to maintain their identity and have paid dearly for their freedom-seeking spirit. However, they have never given up hope of gaining their freedom one day, despite the increasing political risks that have now escalated to genocide. This scenario does not apply in large to Han Chinese and other cultures in China under the same regime.

The survival strategies and instincts of Han Chinese, including Chinese intellectuals, are politically shaped on the surface and culturally refined at a deeper level. This mindset is the result of an interaction between the cultural idealism of antiquity and the political realism of the present. This society encourages social disengagement based on the wisdom of self-protection, while promoting an attitude so controlled, so sophisticated, that no feelings are shown in response to the injustices occurring to or around them. Individuals do not respond to a situation until or unless it happens to them, directly—and even then, they show minimal emotion. This social environment creates a condition where social injustices are committed freely, without fear of being seen or observed by others, because any witnesses will be nothing more than passive bystanders. Individuals are not left with any strong memories of what occurred and will feel no urge or obligation to track down the culprit. Within this social and political milieu, the CCP is defiantly operating concentration camps, with Han Chinese citizens acting as disinterested bystanders at best and perpetrators at worst.

This indifference sounds cruel, although culturally seen as a looking inward that allows one to build up the mental strength and capacity to resist the external world in the most natural way. Cruelty is masked by virtue of indifference, which justifies non-action in any unnatural situation. It is not simply the manifestation of deeply entrenched self-protection, but something more disturbing at a deeper level.

As an example, I would like to consider the use of the word that means "to kill you" or "to beat you to death" (打死你), which is a common expression that appears in jokes, while scolding a child, or when mildly or severely threatening somebody in Chinese society. It is a kind of linguistic profanity that Chinese use much as Americans use the "F-word," frequently and widely in almost any context. I find the frequent use of this word in Chinese culture both interesting and concerning. When I was a child, each time I heard this word used for anything, big or small, significant or insignificant, I felt strangely amused and then immediately terrified. For in my culture, Uyghur culture, we could only use terminology like "to beat you" when we are angry and very serious. We would never easily use the word "to kill," which is a social taboo. The use of this expression in different contexts across cultures still fascinates me. I observed many aspects of Han Chinese and their society over the years, including their use of this expression. I found that it is not merely a linguistic habit, but also a socio-psychological habit—one that helps release inner tension and stress in a society where people are afraid to reveal themselves at the expense of losing face or being ridiculed, excluded, and punished.

In this shame-averse society, people avoid being each other's mirror as part of the essential teachings of Confucius, preferring to be introverted and suppress their emotions, whenever possible. These suppressed emotions accumulate and fester over time, waiting for an appropriate occasion and outlet for release. When the time is right and proper, this expression can serve as a perfect way to air their feelings strongly but safely. The emphasis on the word meaning, "to kill" offers an ideal opportunity for instant satisfaction by externalizing the illusion of killing, releasing all negative energy associated with it in their mind.

However, the indiscriminate use of this expression within a variety of contexts points to it being something more disturbing than just a form of mild neuroticism. First, the habit trivializes the seriousness of the act of killing. Even Chinese intellectuals use it in their daily lives, normalizing it without thinking seriously about possible consequences. They know this kind of expression is widely condoned and will be properly understood. Nobody takes it seriously or is offended because everybody uses it very loosely. As such, Han Chinese have developed a strange sense of indifference, not only to this particular expression, but also to its real-world application. The loose and indiscriminate use of the terminology creates an emotional insensitivity to it.

By way of explanation, let me turn to *Diary of a Madman* (狂人日记) written by Lu Xun, a leftist Chinese writer famous for his chilling criticism of Chinese culture, society, mentality, and customs. Written just before the May Fourth Movement in 1919, which heralded a new era of modern China politically and of the New Culture Movement culturally, the novel reads as a critical literary text. He addressed the increasing tension between old and new, medievalism (feudalism) and modernity, Confucianism and self-critical Chinese consciousness, and collective guilt and redemption. As the title suggests, the story is a fragmented and possibly delusional account of a paranoiac insular villager, who suspects the widespread practice of cannibalism, attributable not only to his neighboring villagers, but also to his own brother. Because of his frightening observations, he investigates the practice, tracing it back 4000 years to the time when the flowers of Chinese civilization were first sprouting. This time in history was shaped by Confucianism, and its idealistic values of virtue and morality, eventuating into horrific cannibalism:

> Everything requires careful consideration if one is to understand it. In ancient times, as I recollect, people often ate human beings, but I am rather hazy about it. I tried to look this up, but my history has no chronology, and scrawled all over each page are the words: "Virtue and Morality." Since I could not sleep anyway, I read intently half the night, until I began to see words between the lines, the whole book being filled with the two words— "Eat people."[9]

Through his depiction of Confucian virtue and morality manifesting in reality as cannibalism, Lu Xun offers one of the most nightmarish, daring, and alarming criticisms of traditional Chinese culture. He is insinuating that by its very nature it forces people to kill each other and, further, represents China as a psychotic space, where even the closest of people are afraid of each other. There was a blatant risk of being eaten, not just by a stranger, even by your own brothers. Nobody is trustworthy or safe in such an environment, where everyone is at war against each other, regardless of affiliation.

This story has a more profound meaning than the surface tale about a quasi-schizophrenic man suffering from delusions of persecution. It is not simply a story of collective insanity within an iron house, a post-apocalyptic metaphorical reference to traditional Chinese society and even to contemporary Chinese society under the spell of the CCP. It is all about radical, though satirical, yearning for reform, revolution, and rebirth, set within a country suffering from false ideals that have secretly allowed leeway for persecution and murder. It also illustrates a certain optimism, placing hope in a new generation that might one day break away from the Chinese tradition that leaves no room for individualism, transparency, or freedom of thought, as expressed in the final sentence: "Perhaps there are still children who have not eaten men? Save the children . . ."

The desperate plea of Lu Xun to save the children who are not yet affected by a culture of cannibalism fell on deaf ears. No one moved to save the Uyghur students who peacefully protested in 1984 and again in 1988 on the streets of Urumqi to claim more rights and freedoms, as expressed in the autonomy law of China. The same attitude prevailed when Chinese students gathered in front of Tiananmen Square to demand more transparency, democracy, and free speech in China. The second coming after the May Fourth Movement and June Fourth Movement (六四民运) in 1989 was a radical attempt of a new generation, possibly as imagined by Lu Xun, to accomplish what was not accomplished in his time: ending political cannibalism and embracing political humanism.

Between 1982 and 1987, there were protests in the streets of Urumqi that, conveniently for the CCP, were considered less newsworthy. During the leadership of Hu Yaobang, Uyghur university students protested against the unfair treatment of Uyghurs, citing it as a breach of the Regional Ethnic Autonomy Law of China. This law promises "the state's full respect for and guarantee of ethnic minorities' right to administer their internal affairs and its adherence to the principle of equality, unity and common prosperity for all nationalities."[10] As a result of the Chinese central and regional governments' unwillingness to enforce this law, Uyghurs experienced a gradual erosion of these rights, which led to the university students' protests. The students' demands included the cessation of restrictions on the linguistic expressions of Uyghurs, a halt to the massive influx of Han Chinese into East Turkistan, the immediate closure of nuclear testing sites in Lopnur and other areas, and greater transparency on the transferring of natural resources from East Turkistan into inner China. The CCP straightforwardly rejected these demands, and student leaders, who organized these protests, were punished by authorities. The Tiananmen Square Student Movements in 1989 marked the end of this quasi-liberalism in the 1980s. Protesting the CCP had become too inherently dangerous, and the Chinese now saw that they risked being killed *en masse* for speaking out.

The suppression of the Uygur voice has never stopped and has further escalated into the current genocide. Now, the victims of the camps paint a darker picture, claiming that torture is prevalent, and the experience is "worse than death."[11] Other reports indicate that there is a widespread practice of organ harvesting, targeting Uyghur inmates.[12] All slaughter of Uyghurs, both inside and outside of the concentration camps, is conducted under the cover of humanitarian assistance. For Lu Xun, the cannibalistic culture was conducted under the name of virtue and morality based on distorted ideals of Confucianism. For Uyghurs today, the current political genocide is conducted under the name of assistance, support, and progress based on the distorted ideology of the CCP.

The disturbing fact is that this cannibalistic political practice is still operative in the broader Chinese society as it is in the concentration camps. In most cases, average Chinese citizens pretend that it does not exist, or it exists only in small parts of Chinese society. However, it still exists not in a physical but an ideological shape. A group of communists—who defend the vital interests of the party which, in turn, protects their vital interests—are still introducing violence to others who may or may not fully conform to this very ideology. This mutual protection safeguards the rule of the dominant party over the rest of the people while maintaining a veil of secrecy. If anybody reveals the suppressed truth about cannibalism, they will immediately be labeled either insane or a liar. Therefore, there are only two options for the madman: choose to pretend that the eating of men is not happening or commit suicide so that they may eat your flesh without feeling guilty that they have killed you.

NOTES

1. Emmanuel Levinas, *Nine Talmudic Readings* (Bloomington: Indiana University Press, 1994), 25.

2. China Change, "A Call for a UN Investigation, and US Sanctions, on the Human Rights Disaster Unfolding in Xinjiang," China Change, August 10, 2018, https://chinachange.org/2018/08/10/a-call-for-a-un-investigation-and-us-sanctions-on-the-human-rights-disaster-unfolding-in-xinjiang/.

3. Wang Lixiong, "Excerpts from 'My West China and Your East Turkestan'—My View on the Kunming Incident," March 3, 2014, https://chinachange.org/2014/03/03/excerpts-from-my-west-china-your-east-Turkistan-my-view-on-the-kunming-incident/.

4. Lin Yutang, *My Country and My People* (London: William Heineman LTD, 1936), 224-225.

5. Radio Free Europe/Radio Liberty, "Uyghur Man Stabbed to Death in South China," January 09, 2010, https://www.rferl.org/a/Uyghur_Man_Stabbed_To_Death_In_South_China/1924768.html.

6. Will Kymlicka and Baogang He, *Multiculturalism in Asia* (Oxford: Oxford University Press, 2005), 59, https://doi.org/10.1093/0199277621.001.0001.

7. Lin Yutang, 56.

8. Lin Yutang, 46.

9. Yunte Huang, ed., *The Big Red Book of Modern Chinese Literature: Writings from the Mainland in the Long Twentieth Century* (New York: W.W. Norton & Company, 2016).

10. "Regional Ethnic Autonomy Law of the People's Republic of China," Congressional-Executive Commission on China, Amended February 28, 2001, https://www.cecc.gov/resources/legal-provisions/regional-ethnic-autonomy-law-of-the-peoples-republic-of-china-amended.

11. Yeni Şafak, "Chinese Internment Camps are 'Torture Centers Worse than Death,' Say Survivors" (last modified December 8, 2018), https://www.yenisafak.com/en/world/chinese-internment-camps-are-torture-centers-that-are-worse-than-death-say-survivors-3468651.

12. CJ Werleman, "New Horrors: China Harvesting Muslim Organs in Concentration Camps," Extra Newsfeed, April 6, 2019, https://extranewsfeed.com/new-horrors-china-harvesting-muslim-organs-in-concentration-camps-9a252d3c373e?gi=f0b0ef3019e.

Chapter Five

Break Your Generations, Break Your Roots

It was such an ordinary evening in 2014. I was having dinner with my friends in their home in Sydney when, suddenly, I received a phone call from China. I answered it, and a man—possibly a Chinese man—began speaking to me in Chinese. He began by introducing himself as somebody from the Xinjiang government with the surname Ma. Immediately, I felt awful as I surmised he was probably a Chinese security agent. He told me that he and his colleagues had visited my home in Atush to see my mother recently, who they believed to be ill. My mind was busy frantically analyzing his message from all perspectives. To me, this sounded like a veiled trick or a mind game. Unlike most games, this one was unfair from the outset, given the fact that my mother, siblings, relatives, and friends back home were all in their hands. He could use this leverage to play the game against me deviously as he wished. If he had an Achille's heel, I might eventually uncover it, but my weakness was already known. My vulnerability lay not in my heel, but in my heart— the heart that began beating irregularly when the man spoke about my mother, whom I had not seen for over fifteen years. At that moment, I felt that it was of utmost importance for me not to let him hear the rapid beatings of my heart over the phone.

Regaining my self-control, I immediately prepared myself for what was coming after this opening remark. The man went on to say they had visited my mother to demonstrate their concern for her well-being. Instantly, I got the point; he was playing a typical carrot-and-stick game. First, a carrot is offered, and then a stick. It is all familiar to me. I responded to him politely, "You don't need to look after her, as she is an experienced medical doctor who knows how to take good care of herself." "No," he replied hurriedly, as a Chinese way of showing care and compassion, "it is our duty to look after her." I became nervous, as the care and compassion carried a double meaning: an overt act of genuine caring and a subtle, covert threat to "take care of" someone in a much more menacing way. I told him calmly, without revealing my edginess, "Leave her alone, as she is fully capable of looking after herself." He replied, "Oh, we do it for the sake of our friendship." Surprised, I asked him, "Friendship? What do you mean by that?" He sounded irritated, "Friendship is friendship, and we are friends."

I paused and looked at my friends, a couple who were attentively listening to the conversation in silence. "No, no," I insisted, as my inherent stubbornness kicked in, "we are not friends, and never will be." He sounded impatient, surprised, and a bit offended, "What are we then, not a friend at all?" I was utterly blunt and uncompromisingly straightforward, "We are enemies, yes, we are." The man sounded increasingly angry as he insisted, "No, no, we are friends!" I replied, "No, never. While you are killing my people, destroying my culture, we can't be friends. We are eternal enemies."

Now all the cards were on the table, and he became impolite and impatient. I prepared to face the music. This time, he trampled the carrot and reached out for a stick, threatening me with the intent of inducing my good behavior, as we began the second scene of this psychological drama. We had reached the stage of the stick: the punishment after the reward failed to achieve its intended purpose.

The man on the other end of the phone changed his tone, and his voice became hoarse, "You must be mistaken that we are enemies. We are friends. Besides, don't forget that we are looking after your mother here."

His pretentious mask slipped from his face, and his true agenda of subduing me and stopping my anti-CCP activities came to the fore.

"You know me," I shot back, "I will not back down from what I have been doing. If you touch a hair of hers, then you will get more resistance out of me, as I will do everything I can here to defend her. So, don't play with me. Remember, I can't be befriended by murderers."

That was the end of my calculated patience and hence of my interest in continuing the conversation with him, so I hung up on him abruptly. His croaky voice disappeared from my world for a while; however, it still came back to haunt me as a vague background voice until it eventually faded away completely.

My heart was still racing, and my emotions surged as I grasped the deeper meaning of the conversation once more. Concern for my mother's well-being filled me with anxiety, as did thoughts of my siblings and others who were so dear to me. I knew well that communication with Chinese security agents is costly for any Uyghurs in exile, but even more so for their family back home.

As I had dreaded and expected from that conversation, I have not been able to contact my mother from that day forward. Somebody told me, later that year, that he heard my mother had publicly denounced me as her son. I tried to call her several times, but I was unsuccessful. Finally, in 2016, I sent her a gift for her birthday, arranging somebody who could visit her privately and deliver it. Later on, I heard that my mother refused to accept the gift, confirming that our relationship as mother and son had ceased to exist for her. Therefore, I was instructed to refrain from bothering her in the future.

I was my mother's only son, along with my three sisters. In Uyghur culture, a son to a mother is a sun to the earth. She devoted her youth to me during a tumultuous relationship with my father, which eventually ended in divorce. To protect me, she did not get married for a long time, telling me she was afraid to lose me emotionally in a new marriage. She often told me that in this world, there were only two people important to her—herself and me. Her second marriage was not as successful as the first one, and in it, she revealed her deepest fragility to me. She was unhappy, agonized, but kind and determined. If I inherited anything biologically from her, it is her relentless determination, dark humor, deep compassion, and subtle pessimism. In 1989, when I was preparing for a university entrance exam in my hometown in Atush, she asked me not to go to a university too far from her so that she could still see me now and again. At that time, I was planning to study at a prestigious Chinese university in Beijing or Shanghai. However, I felt that I could not refuse her plea, as I was aware that I was the only happiness she had ever had in her life. I agreed to study at Kashgar Normal Institute that year. The first time I entered this university, a deep sense of regret occupied my heart. Yet, I continued to study there, for the sake of the close emotional relationship to and proximity with my mother.

Against her wishes, I chose to work at a publishing house in Urumqi, the capital city of East Turkistan, after I graduated from university in 1993. She was distraught. On the day I was leaving for Urumqi, she came into my room, sobbing. She looked me in the eyes and said, barely audibly, "I have raised a little bird in my palm for over the past 22 years with my utmost devotion, love, and sacrifice, and today this bird is about to fly away from me. And I don't know when I can see it again." It was the most heartbreaking moment of my life. My heart was so heavy, and I felt that I was abandoning her to her bitter loneliness, betraying her love.

During my life in Urumqi, which was a much more cosmopolitan and Han-Chinese centric city, I witnessed the gradual deterioration of social, economic, and political life of Uyghurs. One day in 1997 after the Ghulja massacre, I told my close friends, "It will be just a matter of time before we are slaughtered by Han Chinese mercilessly. This will be the last peaceful time for us, perhaps." My friends all vehemently disagreed with my opinion. Some of them showered their scorn on me, saying that I am a pessimist and too biased to see the real progress in the life of Uyghurs.

"How do you know that we are going to be killed by them?" they demanded. I hesitantly replied, "I cannot prove it argumentatively or scientifically. Nor can I show you any document that says so. However, I can tell you that I have learned their long history at the request of my father. Besides, I have looked deep into their eyes, which are full of piercing hatred towards us all, silently telling us that we have no place in their occupied space. This hatred is not normal. It is something strangely transhistorical and transcendental. You can find this hatred in the eyes of almost all Han Chinese that you encounter. It seems to me that they are just waiting for the right time to leach out their hatred to us massively. I cannot continue to stay in China. I should either go overseas or to wait to be arrested and killed here. I have to save myself from this imminent risk." They called me an idealist and a doomsayer. Sadly, nobody believed me. I also knew that for them to be immersed in a deep sleep, oblivious to the nature of their reality, was as painful as the waking up in this reality. Either way, there was a heavy price that we were forced to pay as Uyghurs. I was alone in defending my sad and starkly apocalyptic view, the acceptance of which would force them to accept the unbearable fragility of their life. They were in a dream-state of denial, and I knew they would not enjoy waking up from it in the end.

I seriously believed in what I had said to them. After that point, I started to put my head down and to study English diligently, like a hermit. I cut myself off from my social networks, as I worked on a plan for getting out of China as soon as possible. Finally, in 2000, I was accepted into Katholieke Universiteit Leuven in Belgium and successfully gained a free life.

All this took place over several years, but it seemed as though it happened too quickly. I had little time to be with my mother. She was confused by my decision to go overseas and, as she saw it, abandon my financial security. I did not try to explain my plan in a detailed way to her. I just told her that I would like to spend some time outside of China, to acquire new knowledge and to fulfill my innate curiosity.

In my university life, my mother encouraged me a lot. She was a great help to me emotionally when I faced so many challenges in Belgium. However, the deepest level of communication with her ceased, as I knew the Chinese security agents were monitoring our telephone communication. Accordingly, I limited myself to telling her about my life in Belgium on a superficial level. This was such a painful period for me and was so difficult to endure. I felt as if I was lying to her about everything: the danger of her and my siblings' situation, and the reality of her world, with which she would have no other option than to be content.

My mother frequently asked me when I could return to her after graduation. Hearing this question was difficult for me, as I knew that I would never go back to that hostile world, where I would quickly end up depressed, dead, or in prison. Studying in Belgium had given me a more objective perspective on China, its ambition, its prosperity, and—above all—its aggression towards Uyghurs, Tibetans, Taiwanese, and towards other countries. This new awareness strengthened my determination not to return home; instead, I would stay abroad to fight against the most horrific organization that humanity has ever been exposed to—the CCP. One day, on the phone, I finally told my mother that I would not return to her. She was gravely silent, sighing, and finally said to me, "I knew it. But I respect your decision as I love you. Do whatever is suitable for you." I was a bit baffled. I expected her to cry, but she was so calm that I could sense her inherent determination and sharp mindedness, although only her breathing was audible, in and out . . .

My predictions sadly were made real in 2009, following the Urumqi riots. After this tragic event, my conversations with my mother became more monotonous and superficial, as we could not engage ourselves in deep interactions at an emotional level, as a mother and her son should. Our conversations became less frequent, as both of us felt the burden of surveillance and the hardship of life in a surveillance state. Finally, I received the call from the Chinese security agent, who threatened me with the prospect of doing my mother harm if I would not stop my anti-China activities. I refused, at the cost of abandoning my mother, siblings, and friends to a situation full of hatred, aggression, retaliation, and violence.

It was emotionally painful for me to accept this form of punishment. Nothing could hurt me more than ending my relationship with my beloved mother, on top of what I can only imagine them doing to her as punishment, directly. I felt as if I was drifting slowly and painfully away from my childhood, home, confidence, and love. In short, I was losing everything she gave me and everything that kept me alive spiritually, making me feel loved, loving, and grounded in this world. I was utterly devastated and disoriented. The name "mother," which is associated with two foundational things in a Uyghur's cultural life, mother tongue and motherland, was taken away from me brutally, leaving me in emotional turbulence, without consolation or cultural reference to my identity. I plunged into emotional chaos, losing my sense of who I was and what I was doing. I was enveloped with bitterness over the absurdity in my situation. My mother paid a heavy price, simply for being my mother, as she was forced to sever her relationship with me under the threat of the CCP. Likewise, I was forced to acknowledge the CCP's heinous power as our blood relationship was mutilated, and my heart was wrenched from within. The CCP can reach out and break any relationships formed in my life, with family or friends, and can destroy everything that signifies who I am. By destroying the primordial links—biological, emotional, and social—that any human would cherish, they tried to push me over the edge.

The Chinese intelligence service expected to cause an emotional breakdown, to break me, by destroying my relationship with my mother. The alternative would be to "fix" me by turning me into their slave, into being a spy for them, with no other option than to assist them in silently and resolutely killing more Uyghurs. The heinous face of this crime was so obvious. It was a deliberate attempt to use my faithfulness to my mother to force me to be faithful to them. They would force me to abandon the first faithfulness if I wished to reject the second faithfulness, which would be too costly for me. Ultimately, I would be "faithless" in the end, regardless of the option I chose.

Accordingly, I became an "ungrateful" son for my mother as I became "ungrateful" to the CCP. The CCP uses this ruse cunningly, as a primary tactic in all manner of emotional manipulations of Uyghurs in exile in similar situations. The Chinese intelligence service continues to play with us, implanting the notion of ungratefulness in our minds, which creates a huge sense of guilt. Under this weight, many Uyghurs have chosen to work for the Chinese, thus exposing themselves to another kind of guilt as they sell out their fellow people to Chinese intelligence. These Uyghurs have lost their freedom and their conscience, controlled by the Chinese intelligence service's mastery of this inescapable array of guilt. This method is one that many Chinese security agents have used to recruit Uyghur spies, both domestically and overseas.

While I viewed myself as determined and compassionate, I was broken deep inside, weeping silently and waking up to a harsh, new reality. I learned that to be an enemy to a state far more sophisticated and powerful, you must be ready to lose what is most dear to you in the hope of one day regaining your dignity and freedom. To fight against this inhuman state, you must prepare to make inhuman decisions to avoid becoming complicit in even more inhuman crimes. If you sell your soul to this monstrous system, the conscience that guides you to conform to your sense of right and wrong may give way to the inherent wrongdoing of this system through intimidation, manipulation, and violence. If you choose to align with this system, it will gradually take each human emotion from you, including your faithfulness to your mother and, more fundamentally, to yourself. It will turn you into a useful tool, as emotionless and cold-hearted as possible, to mercilessly silence and punish another fellow human being dear to you. Ultimately, I refused this challenge of my faithfulness to my mother only to save my conscience, in defiance against this system, by refusing my loyalty to the CCP.

After that, I did not receive any more phone calls from Chinese security agents. There was nothing but a corrosive, soul-destroying silence. I have had no news about my mother since then. Not one day has passed without me missing her, who denounced me against her will and who showed her immense love in denouncing me as well. In gradually separating from my mother to continue my advocacy against the CCP, I went through an experience of rediscovering love in its utter destruction, seeming betrayal, and ultimate disappearance from my life, perhaps for good.

Many journalists have interviewed me about this experience since it happened. Their questions ultimately trend in the same direction: "Do you feel any sense of regret in dedicating yourself to the cause of your people, which cost you your mother and her love?" However logical these questions might sound, I inevitably feel a surge of irritation as my initial, silent reaction. How could I weigh in on the gravity of these conflicting duties? There is my filial duty for my innocent mother and siblings, who doubtlessly face merciless punishment because of my actions against this inhuman regime. Moreover, there is my duty for my motherland, currently under the heel of these same tormentors.

After a long pause, I usually answer them in a way that fully satisfies me, "These two duties are not incompatible because they are intertwined in such a way that they presuppose each other at the deepest level possible. I learned how to love my motherland through enjoying the infinite love of my mother and learned how to love my mother unconditionally through dedicating myself wholeheartedly to my motherland." Usually, they would then pressure me to be more specific: "What if you are forced to choose only one option over the other?"

This pressure forces me to revisit the painful experience of losing my relationship with my mother. I generally reply, "If that is the case, I would choose my duty for my nation for the simple reason that my mother would not feel safe if I am not safe in my own nation. Therefore, this naturally requires that I should first dedicate myself to the freedoms of my nation, then all Uyghur mothers, including my mother, will be able to feel free and safe."

BREAKING UP FAMILIES–UYGHURS IN EXILE

The CCP is determined to destroy Uyghurs through their family connections, not only in implementing the Four Breaks, but also by independently attacking these connections on an individual basis. An example of this is the fate that recently befell thousands of Uyghur students in Egypt. In July 2017, Egyptian security forces arrested dozens of Uyghurs who were studying at the famous Islamic Al-Azhar University in Egypt. A further seventy Uyghurs were arrested in Nasr City and twenty more at Borg El Arab airport in Alexandra, all of whom were believed to be delivered to the Chinese authorities and expatriated back to China.[1] Other Uyghur students received phone calls from their parents back home who, under duress from the Chinese security forces, told them to return to China immediately. Upon their arrival, they were arrested, disappeared, or killed.

I heard the same story from other Uyghur students who escaped from Egypt to Turkey, seeking refuge there. They spoke of the many students in Egypt who could not refuse the demands of their parents, knowing that if they did, then their parents would pay a heavy price for it. They were beset by the same moral dilemma I had faced—either to listen to their parents as a loyal child, as their culture had taught them, or to refuse with a determination not to return. Ultimately, it was clear to them that if they returned, they could not save either themselves or their parents, but the dilemma went even deeper. To accept the request of their parents meant upholding their values of maintaining the integrity of the family (home). To reject it would mean to act selfishly, abandoning these fundamental values. The former scenario reinforces the family integrity as a vital force that has kept Uyghur families resilient throughout unending upheavals and disasters. This value should arguably be defended at all costs, as it is the foundation of Uyghur identity that is formed and nurtured. The latter option, on the other hand, is a realistic consideration of personal safety, which recognizes the futility of saving parents in a situation where nobody will be safe in the end. Therefore, the former choice is courageous but fatal, whereas the latter one practical but selfish. With the first choice, one takes an informed risk to save something more valuable than one's life, whereas the second choice involves saving one's self at the risk of a permanent and irredeemable sense of guilt.

When examined at a deeper level, the first option is as absurd as the second one. Both, in essence, are a losing proposition. The absurdity of the situation is that the CCP ruthlessly forces everyone to fail, ultimately, regardless of how considerate they were in choosing one option over the other one. There is no good choice available—if they returned, they would perish in the darkness of the camps, and if they did not return, they would be tormented for the rest of their lives by the dark shadow of guilt in their heart.

To accomplish their inhuman plan, the CCP has used our family relationship and filial values against us. Many Uyghurs in Turkey, who refused to go back to China to see their parents, have told me they suffer from nightmares and a sense of survivor's guilt. This guilt is more complicated than survivor's guilt in a usual sense. Uyghurs, who experience the effects of this syndrome, have an added burden of sensing the futility of any efforts that they may resort to, ultimately deeming themselves helpless and hopeless. They are not wondering what would have been different if they were there with their family members, or why they are alive while others are about to perish. Ultimately, they believe that whatever they chose, it would end up in failure. Then, why would they feel guilty? They felt guilty because, in either case, they were forced by their situation to make a self-defeating choice, even though they knew the horrifying result. More absurd is that they could not avoid making a decision, as existentialism teaches, because the hostile regime forces them to choose. As they make their terrible choice, they are aware that by simply being a Uyghur, they and their parents would never be spared by the CCP. It is this fatalistic feeling of guilt, the kismet of Uyghurs, which is inescapable for them.

BREAKING UP FAMILIES AT HOME

Home is a sacred space for Uyghurs, as it is for any other culture in the world. In it, we build our inner world, personalities, habits, dreams, and thoughts. Home is where our cultural values are exchanged, negotiated, and re-enacted through generational communications. It is, ideally speaking, where our fathers establish authority, power, and order while our mothers nurture a sense of love, compassion, and sacrifice. This combination of two indispensable pillars constitutes the rational vigor and emotional richness of our life. Home is a critical social unit, the foundation of social harmony, cohesiveness, and unity. As Confucius said, "The strength of a nation derives from the integrity of the home."

In the colonial reality of living under the CCP, Uyghurs have made the home their emotional and spiritual shelter, in which they can find daily solace from the fear, humiliation, and terror of the outside, Han-Chinese-dominated, world. At home, Uyghurs maintain their innermost privacy, preserving all their most sacred values to pass on to future generations. It is the fortress of Uyghur identity, what they proudly call the second nation, (ئىككىنچى ۋەتەن). Arguably, Uyghurs would already have been destroyed, had they not been able to keep their identity alive in their tiny and gradually diminishing space, their home as the last shrine. Now, the CCP's explicit intent is to destroy systematically Uyghur homes from within, through breaking their generations, roots, connections, and origins. This space, wherein their most primordial sense of safety, belonging, and self-esteem resides, is now slipping away.

The CCP violated this sacred space in 2018 by sending a million government officials, most of whom are Han Chinese, to live in Uyghur homes, observing the life of Uyghurs in the name of creating a harmonious society. Human Rights Watch issued a report on May 13, 2018, entitled *China: Visiting Officials Occupy Homes in Muslim Region: "Becoming Family" Campaign Intensifies Repression in Xinjiang*. This report states that Chinese officials, since early 2018, have imposed regular "home stays" on families in the predominantly Muslim region of Xinjiang. These visits are part of the government's increasingly invasive "Strike Hard" campaign. During these visits, families are required to provide officials with information about their lives and political views and are subjected to political indoctrination.[2]

Treated in this highly intrusive manner, Uyghurs no longer feel safe within their own homes. While their sense of security is shattered, officials carefully observe Uyghurs to ensure they have no problematic ideas that might pose a threat to the CCP. The officials document everything about Uyghurs' lives at home: their cuisine, their daily rhythms, their conversations with each other, their communal engagements, and—above all—their thoughts. Once the CCP had ruthlessly invaded this safe space, it launched its final,

ultimate assault upon Uyghurs—the assault of their minds. The CCP intended to invade Uyghurs' minds so absolutely as to render everything in it
visible. Uyghurs would then no longer have anything to hide, left with nothing resembling the natural internal privacy of individual human beings, ordi-
narily endowed with the capacity to think freely and invisibly. Uyghurs are
rendered observable from every angle, both external and internal, as a pre-
condition for the CCP to declare that the "barbarians" have been destroyed in
their families, communities, and even in their minds.

The political indoctrination that occurs through these intrusive measures
is emotional torture for Uyghurs, who have lost their land, culture, and religion—everything, in the end. Now they are losing themselves in their homes,
in their last private space. They are entrapped inside their homes, along with
the silent observation of surveillance cameras outside, recording their movements with precise accuracy, making their efforts to escape and be invisible
futile, desperate, and dangerous, imprisoned both inside and outside.

The Chinese officials, who were sent by the CCP to live and sleep with
Uyghurs in their homes, could ask anything. The Uyghurs could not refuse to
answer their questions, although some of these questions were too personal.
It is quite disturbing, and I would question the ultimate aim of the CCP's
interest in their lives. Are they satisfied with keeping an eye on these Uyghurs, or do they intend to learn how to behave and think like a Uyghur,
impersonating them one day? If it is the former, then it is a fearsome method
of turning Uyghurs into the subjects of thought control processes in their
most private space. It reinforces yet again that Uyghurs are in the grip of the
omnipresent CCP, who will always hunt them down everywhere. If it is the
latter, then these Han Chinese may intend to emerge after the Uyghurs have
perished completely, showing the world that Uyghurs are not being killed,
but merely replaced with a new type of Uyghur. These new Uyghurs may
speak the Uyghur language, may cook Uyghur food, and may behave like
Uyghurs.

Considering this most sinister possibility, it is not surprising that Han
Chinese in East Turkistan have shown a growing interest in learning Uyghur
dance. Usually, Uyghur dance—especially the Uyghur dance performed by
women—is too difficult for Han Chinese to learn due to its intricate movements, subtle rhythms, cultural nuances, and deep spiritual meaning. Moreover, Han Chinese have never shown any great interest in learning it previously. However, they have recently been very active in performing Uyghur
dance on the streets and in other public places, encroaching on a previously
untouchable cultural space. Now their sudden embrace of it demonstrates
that Han Chinese know there are no more Uyghurs to make them feel culturally inferior, to pass judgment on their clumsy dance, or to reclaim their
cultural heritage.

All this tells us how successful Han Chinese now are in their effort to embody Uyghurs, imitating their dance, one of the most sophisticated Uyghur behavioral manifestations and patterns. They know the Uyghur body is now empty, along with its soul, withering away and dying; therefore, this body is ready to be occupied. Dance is a first and decisive step to fill the space, using the process of cultural appropriation, or a better, more subtle invasion. It is a means of conquering Uyghur culture, to occupy all space Uyghurs have previously claimed as their own. Now the physical space Uyghurs once inhabited has been emptied out, the cultural space of Uyghurs has become empty as well. You do not see Uyghurs on the streets, singing and dancing as before. Some homes and neighborhoods are empty, and Uyghur towns have become ghost towns. Uyghur life has disappeared into the black hole of the concentration camps and prisons.

Han Chinese are now attempting to experience Uyghur culture, not to feel the Uyghurs' pain, but to feel their pride, by impersonating a Uyghur from within. It is a secret pleasure to enjoy being a Uyghur, whom they had long hated and vowed to defeat. They are learning to imitate Uyghur dance to perform it themselves and cover up the fact that Uyghurs are gone for show on official visits in the future.

However, to occupy the body is not enough if the mind is still operative. The Uyghurs' last shred of privacy still exists in their minds, invisible to Chinese communists. The mind is where they may hide their thoughts, feelings, fears, anxiety, hatred, fury, and aspirations. Without occupying this space, the conquest of the 'barbarian' Uyghurs cannot be declared successful.

For a communist, the mind of the masses is nothing but an invisible battlefield to be occupied and managed. To achieve victory in this sphere does not require a bloody battle, but a forced thought reform. Chinese communists have always advocated ideological homogeneity as a means of control, brought about through a series of campaigns to unify the thoughts of the masses. Motivated by the ancient Chinese adage that alterity is a threat, communists aim to eliminate all thoughts not aligned with the CCP.

Further, communists view the mind as a potentially unreliable space, vulnerable to dangerous ideas. Any social change must start with an individual, so all individuals must be controlled. Individuals not currently aligned with the CCP mentality must undergo a profound alteration of their mindset through external intervention, an insertion of communist ideologies into their paradigms and conceptual schemas. Unsurprisingly, communists are ever suspicious of people's minds, the invisible repositories of dangerous ideas and anti-revolutionary thoughts. These opaque spaces may harbor not just anti-communist tendencies, but the will to overthrow the establishments and communist super-structure.

All ideologies are rooted in a firm belief in the absolute correctness of their one system of ideas, thoughts, and behavior, maintaining that they have the answer for any question, the solution to any challenge. This uncompromising belief, by its very nature, does not tolerate other systems of thought, considering them to be not only erroneous but an outright threat to their existence. This means that any such ideology is a mixture of conflicting parts, both invincible and vulnerable at once. An extreme ideology is a dysfunctional marriage between the firm belief in its supremacy over other systems on the one hand, and an abiding paranoia about the attractiveness of these other systems, and their potential to seduce its followers, on the other. It is a paradoxical mixture of complete trust and an extreme simultaneous lack of trust.

This paradox explains why communist regimes are historically vulnerable to deep paranoia, which motivates them to ruthlessly eradicate their own followers until they feel safe. This paranoia leaves communist ideologists restless, fearful, and suspicious. When intensified, it manifests as uncontrollable anxiety that leads them to perpetrating more drastic and cruel methods of torture to delve deep into the minds of the people. For example, Stalin purged prominent party members of the Soviet Communist Party at its height, being suspicious that some of them might subvert the party from within because of dangerous and seductive influences. Mao Zedong performed the same selective elimination during the Cultural Revolution, based on his fear that revisionists were controlling the CCP. He believed that his leadership was at risk, primarily due to his disastrous economic decisions, which brought about economic chaos and widespread famine, causing the death of millions of Chinese people. This trend currently continues through Xi Jinping's anti-corruption campaign, which began shortly after the 18th National Congress in 2012.

Communists believe the origin of any ideological mistake in action does not lie in behavior, but in thoughts. Any social reform should therefore focus on thought reform, which will then bring about behavioral reform. This behavioral reform is one of the primary objectives of establishing the concentration camps.

As part of their psychological warfare, the methods that Chinese authorities use inside the camps are coercive, including political indoctrination, ideological purges, and mass propaganda. Detainees are forced to learn Mandarin Chinese and Chinese law by heart, listen to political lectures, sing hymns praising the CCP and Xi Jinping, and write self-confessional reports. Failure to cooperate results in heavy punishment.

In addition, detainees are permitted to use only a specific prescribed set of words, with a view to taking control of the contents of their thoughts, perceptions, and even feelings. As Wittgenstein said, "The limits of my language mean the limits of my world." In the end, the thought process of a detainee can operate only in a tightly restricted area, where there is no novelty, but only endless repetitions. Repetitive thoughts eventually become meaningless and self-referential, signifying the total surrender of the mind to the will of its captors.

Communist "doctors" in the camps believe, or at least pretend to believe, that they are abiding by the Hippocratic Oath's promise to "First do no harm" as they treat Uyghur thought-patients. They have been conditioned to believe they are not causing any harm to their patients; on the contrary, it is beneficial for them to be ideologically, if not medically, healthy. In fact, they likely believe the patients they treat are not even aware of their own problems, and some patients are simply too stubborn to admit they are ideologically sick. Therefore, it is the physician's moral duty to convince them that they are sick and in need of medical treatment. Of course, only communist doctors can cure them of their particular sickness.

The doctors' deluded belief in the benign nature of their task is so firmly rooted that they approach their responsibilities very seriously and diligently. To resist their aid is a sign, not of sanity, but of insanity. Any lack of appreciative cooperation serves to support the thought-patients diagnosis and shows how a hardline approach to it is more justified than ever. In the end, the doctors' unwavering belief in the virtue of their approach only shows that they are as psychologically disturbed and in need of care as are the thought-patients they intend to cure. They are as brainwashed as Uyghurs in this situation—all victims of the same political ideology. The consequence of their thought control is such that they cannot see they are also thought patients, who have lost the meaning of their actions.

The devastating impact of re-education campaigns is not only felt by Uyghur detainees, but by their broken families. These campaigns have further destroyed Uyghur families, which constitute the most delicate fabric of Uyghur society. Uyghur families are the foundational social fortification against the ongoing assault of Sinicization or forced cultural assimilation by Han Chinese. The separation of children from parents who enter the camps has caused enormous, possibly irreparable damage to Uyghur families.

Chris Buckley described this damage alarmingly in an article in the *New York Times*, entitled: "China Is Detaining Muslims in Vast Numbers. The Goal: 'Transformation'" as follows:

> The mass internments also break Uyghur families by forcing members to disown their kin or by separating small children from their parents. So many parents have been detained in Kashgar, a city in western Xinjiang, that it has expanded boarding schools to take custody of older, "troubled" children.[3]

To highlight this point, let us look at some numbers (albeit approximate, as real figures are not known) that delineate the overall impact of this cultural genocide. In May of 2019, Randall Schriver, who currently leads Asia policy at the US Defense Department, confirmed, "The (Chinese) Communist Party is using the security forces for mass imprisonment of Chinese Muslims in concentration camps." He estimated that the number of detained Muslims could be "closer to 3 million citizens."[4] Let us assume that of the three million Uyghurs being held, only half of them have a single child. One child for every two people is probably a conservative estimate, but it would mean that detainees have left behind 1.5 million children. This is a huge number—and the children are not numbers, but human beings. Where are they now—in orphanages, or disappeared, or in boarding schools? In the end, for every person that is detained, at least three other family members will be affected, totaling approximately nine to eleven million individuals, including children. Chinese government's statistics give the population of Uyghurs as more than eleven million. If this figure is accurate, then every Uyghur in East Turkistan is affected by the CCP policy to break the roots of the Uyghur population, thoroughly, systematically, and permanently.

The separation of the children from their parents is a blatant implementation of the Four Breaks, intended to break the most delicate connections that make us human, the bond of a child to their parents. These bonds give children a primordial sense of safety, self-esteem, identity, and belonging, vital to establishing their personality. Now, all this is being destroyed, leaving this new generation in darkness. Where once the edifice of their heart was supported by two pillars—mother as the source of love and compassion and father as the source of authority and order—now, the pillars have collapsed and the edifice has crumbled, leaving only trauma.

The children are now raw, their mind a *tabula rasa* for the communists to engineer in any way that they wish. They can perform any kind experiment on them, forcing them to denounce either their parents, as I experienced, or their Uyghur nationality, culture, and religion. The communists steal their hearts by stealing them from their parents and family. Profoundly broken, they go through any cruelty without being able to conceptualize its meaning. When learning this history one day, they will see themselves as a stolen and broken generation, destined to carry this sense of shame, trauma, and eternal bitterness with them for the rest of their life. That is, they cannot comprehend the meaning of this separation from their parents at this stage, or the trauma inscribed in their innocent hearts like a scar on their face. The scar grows with them and never goes away, reminding them of their life without parental love: abandoned, humiliated, and brutalized. If they are in orphanages or institutions, their trauma will endure as they are subject to a systematic controlling process. Alone in this world, they feel eventually that their trauma will only become more deeply embedded and more powerful with time.

NOTES

1. Mohamed Mostafa and Mohamed Nagi, "'They Are Not Welcome': Report on the Uyghur Crisis in Egypt," Association of Freedom of Thought and Expression October, Egyptian Commission for Rights and Freedoms, October 1, 2017, https://afteegypt.org/en/academ ic_freedoms/2017/10/01/13468-afteegypt.html.

2. Human Rights Watch, "China: Visiting Officials Occupy Homes in Muslim Region," Human Rights Watch, May 13, 2018, https://www.hrw.org/news/2018/05/13/china-visiting-officials-occupy-homes-muslim-region.

3. Chris Buckley, "China Is Detaining Muslims in Vast Numbers. The Goal: 'Transformation,'" *New York Times*, September 8, 2018, https://www.nytimes.com/2018/09/08/world/asia/china-uighur-muslim-detention-camp.html.

4. Phil Stewart, "China Putting Minority Muslims in 'Concentration Camps,' U.S. Says," Reuters, May 3, 2019, https://www.reuters.com/article/us-usa-china-concentrationcamps/china-putting-minority-muslims-in-concentration-camps-us-says-idUSKCN1S925K.

Chapter Six

Two-Facedness and Ideological Viruses

Truth is so obscure in these times, and falsehood so established, that, unless we love the truth, we cannot know it.

—Blaise Pascal

In this chapter, I will explain the anatomy of China's repressive policies against Uyghur intellectuals in particular and Uyghurs in general. I will also focus on the variety of excuses the CCP finds to justify the establishment of concentration camps and to rationalize its systematic attempts at eliminating Uyghur cultural elites.

TWO-FACEDNESS OF UYGHUR INTELLECTUALS

Two-facedness is an ancient Chinese concept derived from a real story that took place during the Yuan Dynasty. It is defined in Chinese culture as a dissonance between action and intention or a lack of firm position on principles, akin to the meaning of "hypocrisy." In essence, it is a form of duplicity revealing something overtly while concealing something else covertly. In creating a sense of ambiguity, it gives rise to the confusion of double standards. This ambiguity defies the demand for a single, absolute definition of truth, and instead leaves it deliberately undefined. It serves the purpose of a social self-defense mechanism as a form of survivalism in a world where nothing is certain or predictable. In an oppressive society where the thoughts, aspirations, and dreams of people are monitored under the pretense of concern for the public's wellbeing, people tend to be ambiguous in revealing themselves. Currently in China, Han Chinese use social ambiguity to cope with political uncertainty and restrictions on their freedom of expression, despite it creating a degree of confusion for others.

The two-facedness of Chinese mannerisms was cheerfully described in a book by *The New Yorker*'s Evan Osnos, citing how publisher Lu Jinbo referenced the Chinese blogger, Han Han:

> In China, our culture forces us to say things that we don't really think. If I say, "Please come over to my place for dinner today," the truth is I really don't want you to come. And you'll say, "You are too kind, but I have other arrangements." This is the way people are used to communicating, whether it's leaders in the newspapers or regular people. All Chinese people understand that what you say and what you think often don't match up. [1]

This linguistic practice is deeply ambiguous, manifesting conflicting expressions and is logically unsound, despite being culturally proper. Sentences usually have two kinds of meaning—one is linguistic, and the other is well-hidden and only decipherable to a person familiar with Chinese culture. As such, they do not both correspond to reality, and internal thoughts often contradict external dialogue. Comments often allude to their opposite. In such a society, any sentence within the context of social customs and norms presents a situation in which these two meanings can be simultaneously both true and false. Despite this contradiction, or possibly because of it, Chinese society operates efficiently and effectively, albeit with an unusual degree of complexity.

Understandably, this practice has its political advantages in the totalitarian state of China, where speech and thought are always censored. It is closely tied to the Chinese "face," a unique concept that is culturally saturated with multilayered meanings, as Han Chinese intellectual Lin Yutang stated, "It is not a face that can be washed or shaved, but a face that can be 'granted' and 'lost' and 'fought for' and 'presented as a gift' . . . Abstract and intangible, it is yet the most delicate standard by which Chinese social intercourse is regulated." [2]

Pragmatically, this cultural practice "saves" the face of Han Chinese by allowing them to take advantage of the ambiguous nature of the political culture. However, this advantage is a foreign and even dangerous, concept for Uyghurs. The CCP has recently suppressed Uyghur intellectuals in the name of fighting against "two-facedness." The label implies that some Uyghurs show their false faces to the party while hiding their hearts from it, the hearts that secretly beat for Uyghurs. The CCP inherently distrust these intellectuals, who they believe harbor a desire for Uyghur nationalism, an idea China has banned as subversive. The Chinese authorities have declared these intellectuals are not in conformity with the CCP, as there is a disparity between their presented face and their internal heart, hidden from scrutiny.

Any fragment of Uyghur life concealed from the gaze of the CCP creates a deep sense of political paranoia. The CCP is a monopolistic party, controlling everything in China, and they tolerate no ambiguity. Any implied difference or otherness is seen as a threat against the existence of the CCP, and so they remain determined to establish and maintain the uniformity of thoughts, feelings, and allegiances. Ambiguity of the heart manifests in the perplexity of the mind, which may lead a Uyghur to deviate from the "right" pathway of communist political idealism. Any human heart invisible and not knowable to the CCP is a heart that is potentially dangerous and definitely untrustworthy.

While Uyghur intellectuals imitate the established practices of two-facedness, concealing their deviant thoughts from state-sponsored censorship, they cannot disrupt the regulatory forces of this culture. Moreover, they cannot escape the alterity of their political and cultural identity, as it is easily recognizable that they are not Han Chinese. It is permissible for Han Chinese to dutifully practice two-facedness daily, both culturally and politically, so long as it serves the interests of the CCP. However, there is zero tolerance of Uyghurs practicing this two-facedness in the same arena. Instead, their position must always be unambiguous, and so the CCP categorizes them in one of three areas: white, black, or grey. There is no tolerance for the ambiguity identified within the grey area, where supposed separatism, terrorism, or anti-CCP thoughts lie. This state creates anxiety and paranoia in Han Chinese and the CCP and so, unsurprisingly, there is a strong focus on eradicating the grey area. Uyghurs who fall within the white or black area are not considered as problematic for Chinese authorities. On these opposite ends of the spectrum, authorities consider the loyalties or disloyalties of Uyghurs to be evident and their behavior predictable. The grey area is the most confusing and difficult for authorities to manage, and the fluidity of the situation only increases their anxiety. Those within both the white and black areas often blend together, moving from one side or the other into the grey area, or vice versa. The relationship among the three zones becomes structurally intertwined, with different possibilities and profound uncertainties, leading to CCP intolerance of Uyghurs in any area. The CCP's desire to ensure eradication of any grey area often culminates in a strategy of widespread, indiscriminate destruction.

The harsh punishment of Uyghur intellectuals who have no links to terrorism highlights the hidden agenda of the CCP. China's real concern is not alleged links to terrorism. In reality, the apprehensiveness has to do with Uyghur intellectuals' dedication to preserving their cultural identity. The Uyghur intellectuals who lived in the communist era, after the annexation of East Turkistan in 1949, played a particular role in a grand political drama, a sort of character whose personality was controlled, and voice altered. They existed within a complex and challenging power structure, socio-economic setting, and cultural milieu. They were permanently displaced, unstable, and volatile. When the CCP needed them, intellectuals were used as a convenient tool to govern the restless Uyghurs. When they lost their significance, they were disposed of or, at best, simply abandoned. Ordinary Uyghurs opposed to CCP rule had expected that Uyghur intellectuals would defend their inalienable rights, take ethical responsibility, and work to find a solution for the life-and-death challenge they all faced. As the CCP was imposing its will on Uyghur intellectuals, forcing them to be loyal, subservient, and inoffensive, ordinary Uyghurs were hoping they would instead be courageous, compassionate, and sacrificing. Caught between these conflicting expectations and demands, Uyghur intellectuals represented a generation that was politically manipulated, culturally traumatized, and ethically ambivalent.

The fate of Ilham Tohti, a well-known Uyghur economist and outspoken human rights activist, is an example of this. Tohti is one of the most unconventional intellectuals, not only for Uyghurs, but also for Han Chinese in China. He challenged, unequivocally, the accepted norms of the ambiguous use of political language. With rare courage, he honestly and critically questioned authorities and institutions in China over Beijing's draconian policy against Uyghurs under the tokenistic label of autonomy. The uniqueness of Tohti's approach does not lie in the way in which he reminded the CCP of its failed promises of autonomy for Uyghurs. What is unique is the fact that he advocated for a conciliatory society where both Han Chinese and Uyghurs could live in harmony, a political ideal that was brutally rejected by the CCP. The price Ilham Tohti paid for such dissonance was a life sentence in jail for alleged separatism. Despite this, he has been internationally recognized with awards for advocating for human rights in the face of adversity, namely the PEN/Barbara Goldsmith Freedom to Write Award (2014), the Martin Ennals Award (2016), the Vaclav Havel Human Rights Prize (2019), and most recently the Sakharov Prize for Freedom of Thought (2019).[3]

The CCP is crushing ordinary Uyghurs under the guise of combating terrorism and destroying intellectuals accused of supposed "two-facedness." Their ultimate aim is frighteningly simple: to destroy the entire Uyghur cultural elite, while using the highly exaggerated threats of terrorism and two-facedness to justify this cultural genocide to the international community. For Uyghur intellectuals, the CCP's ongoing punishment points to something more alarming: they are no longer considered a useful bridge between ordinary Uyghurs and CCP leaders. This shift foreshadows the eventual destruction of this bridge, shutting down any attempt to manage relations, and further abetting the annihilation of Uyghurs in concentration camps.

Currently, almost all famous Uyghur intellectuals are either sentenced to lengthy jail terms or incarcerated in concentration camps under some highly generalized pretext, due to the CCP's paranoia that they are two-faced. The accusation that one is two-faced is impossible to defend against, and not simply because the CCP is inherently paranoid. Moreover, there is no opportunity to prove the CCP itself is two-faced, although this is certainly the case. This two-facedness is an example of the aforementioned parallel world created by the CCP, using gaslighting to misrepresent what is happening, and giving different interpretations of the same event for domestic and international audiences. The CCP portrays the concentration camps as re-education and vocational learning centers for adults and kindergartens for children, concealing their real purpose as a tool to eliminate Uyghurs, their culture, and their identity. As another example, the CCP justifies its genocide of Uyghurs as a counterterrorism measure (in the parallel world), while actually terrorizing Uyghurs, destroying their hope for their future, self-esteem, dignity, and ultimately their very existence (in the real world).

IDEOLOGICAL VIRUSES

Let me now focus on how China has come up with the idea of the contraction of an ideological virus, a terrorism virus. This was used as the main pretext to justify putting Uyghurs in the camps. In 2018, Human Rights Watch published a comprehensive research-based report on the concentration camps, entitled "Eradicating Ideological Viruses—China's Campaign of Repression against Xinjiang's Muslims," reporting:

> The Xinjiang authorities have made foreign ties a punishable offense, targeting people with connections to an official list of "26 sensitive countries," including Kazakhstan, Turkey, Malaysia, and Indonesia. People who have been to these countries, have families, or otherwise communicate with people there, have been interrogated, detained, and even tried and imprisoned.[4]

Common sense tells us that this is an absurd concept. It presupposes that Islam, or any other religion for that matter, is virus-infested and contagious. Using this theory, if I visit the Vatican, I am in danger of contracting a Catholicism virus. Hypothetically, this being true, the Vatican should first be quarantined, and it should be grateful to China for identifying the existence of a deadly virus within it. A Chinese or a Westerner who visits Saudi Arabia does not contract any ideological virus. If this were the case, those who went to Saudi Arabia should go through a thorough quarantining process. In reality, Islam is not a virus, and even terrorism is not a virus; it is a dangerous ideology that the majority of Muslims do not believe or practice. Despite this conflict with reality, the CCP initially used the terrorism virus theory as the main criteria to incarcerate Uyghurs in concentration camps, providing a justification in their parallel world.

It is no secret that the CCP have been busy finding plausible excuses to justify the heavy-handed punishment of Uyghurs. Twenty years ago, Uy-

ghurs who went to Saudi Arabia were not punished for "contracting an ideological virus," but rather for illegally going to Mecca for a hajj. While the
justification is different, the actions and actors are exactly the same. It is just
as absurd to punish a Muslim for going to hajj, which is part of their religious
duty, as it is to intern them in the camps for contracting an imaginary virus.
However absurd this criterion is, the CCP is still adamantly using it to justify
the internment of Uyghurs, Kazakhs, and other Muslims. The CCP's main
purpose is to instill a fear of the Islamic faith in the minds of Han Chinese. In
addition, they aim not only to justify their own inhuman practices, but to
modify beliefs internationally concerning the appropriate response to terrorism. It is quite scary how successful they have been.

Most Han Chinese still remember the national outbreak of SARS (Severe
Acute Respiratory Syndrome) in Southern China between 2002 and 2003,
which spread to infect 8098 people. The eruption of COVID-19, on the other
hand, that raced through Wuhan before evolving into a worldwide pandemic
caused fear among the Chinese populace, not to mention widespread panic
and chaos around the globe.

The CCP knows that anything likened to a viral outbreak will immediately cause Chinese people to panic. Although the CCP is not openly comparing
the ideological virus to COVID-19, SARS or other diseases at this time, the
underlying psychological effect has been achieved. It is quite simple to incite
panic in the Han Chinese, even using indirect means. By justifying the suppression of Uyghurs with this absurd charge, the CCP can kill two birds with
one stone. They can convince the world that it is reasonable to quarantine the
virus in the minds of Uyghurs by putting them in small, institutionalized
spaces for ideological "disinfection." Just as you would work to disinfect the
body of a person who has contracted a virus, so one must treat a mind
infected with the virus of terrorism, an ideological virus, in the same way.

At the same time, they slander the image of Uyghurs in the minds of Han
Chinese in this vicious process of vilification. As such, Uyghurs are portrayed as ideologically sick so that they must be forcibly separated from the
rest of Han Chinese society. This elicits little to no sympathy from Han
Chinese, as it reinforces the "reasonable precautions" that are being taken. It
also isolates Uyghurs, setting them apart and implying that it is dangerous to
even communicate with them, as they carry an ideological virus as deadly as
a physical one. It is no wonder, then, that Uyghurs are currently experiencing
such extreme racial discrimination, both from the CCP as propagators of this
absurd accusation, and from Han Chinese who believe it.

However absurd their reasoning is, it is an accepted paradigm for execu-
tors under the command of Xi Jinping, the mastermind of the Uyghur genocide. Though he is not visible at the scene of the murders, nor is he issuing
any statement to explain the reasoning for his determined focus on the Uyghur issue, the impression persists, nonetheless. It offers an illusion of rea-

sonableness and necessity and provides a conceptual framework for Han Chinese masses to support this genocide, overtly or covertly. Internationally, it has provided a sense that the whole operation is not arbitrary or chaotic, but is well-prepared, rational, and systematic.

Of course, all absurdities have their limitations in wooing human reason, as does this one; therefore, not everyone will be convinced. However, many horrendous crimes in human history started with something deeply absurd, not with something rational. The point is not just that these crimes are absurd, but that they are well-disguised under a veil of absurdities, preventing human reason from clearly seeing what is behind them. And so, to give Chinese officials additional criteria to indicate who to place in the camps, the CCP came up with this new absurdity to complement and justify their actions.

However, not all Uyghurs incarcerated in the camps have been to one of the 26 countries identified as a place where the virus was said to be contracted. Many are highly respected intellectuals who know Mandarin and Chinese law far better than many Han Chinese, and they are also equipped with far better job skills. However, to cover up the deficiencies of the first absurdity, Chinese authorities are compelled to explain the second absurdity by concealing the truth on the ground—to accuse them of being two-faced. The CCP is incarcerating Uyghur intellectuals for two reasons. Firstly, they are Uyghur Muslims with a rebellious cultural identity and a dangerous religious ambition. Secondly, being highly intelligent, they are the greatest threat to expose the absurdities of the CCP's justifications. Interestingly, to convince the world of these absurd ideas, the CCP must first convince its own people, so that the world may buy into it as well. It does this through brutal and indiscriminate force against any dissonance, a method that has proved very effective.

By means of these absurdities, the CCP has successfully created a smokescreen of Uyghurs who need intervention and quarantine, as a sick person needs medical assistance. It is in the best interest of Uyghurs to accept the intervention voluntarily, to assist with their mental and ideological "wellbeing." In this portrayal, the re-education training is a good option for them, a point that was confirmed by one of the camp inmates: "If I wasn't here studying, I don't even want to imagine where I'd be. Maybe I would have followed those religious extremists into a life of crime. The government and party found me in time and saved me."[5]

Instead of seeing the CCP as a murderer, the inmates are brainwashed into viewing it as a savior. This is nothing short of the ingenuity of the CCP, which is not only exceptional at concealing their crimes, but also at portraying them not as destruction, but as benevolence. This logical next step in the virus absurdity is tantamount to saying that Uyghurs have chosen their "ideological treatment" in the camps voluntarily. Their misery is not the CCP's fault, but their own. Strangely, it can sound logical, as long as one accepts the first premise that Uyghurs are ideologically sick and in need of urgent medical intervention, perhaps up to and including euthanasia.

NOTES

1. Evan Osnos, *Age of Ambition: Chasing Fortune, Truth and Faith in the New China* (New York: Farrar, Straus and Giroux, 2015), 174.

2. Lin Yutang, 190.

3. Mamtimin Ala, "Turn in the Two-Faced: The Plight of Uyghur Intellectuals," *The Diplomat*, October 12, 2018, https://thediplomat.com/2018/10/turn-in-the-two-faced-the-plight-of-uyghur-intellectuals/.

4. Human Rights Watch, "'Eradicating Ideological Viruses': China's Campaign of Repression Against Xinjiang's Muslims," Human Rights Watch, September 9, 2018, https://www.hrw.org/report/2018/09/09/eradicating-ideological-viruses/chinas-campaign-repression-against-xinjiangs.

5. Lily Kuo, "From Denial to Pride: How China Changed Its Language on Xinjiang's Camps," *The Guardian*, October 22, 2018, https://www.theguardian.com/world/2018/oct/22/from-denial-to-pride-how-china-changed-its-language-on-xinjiangs-camps.

Chapter Seven

Morality of Genocide

PSYCHOLOGICAL ASPECTS OF GENOCIDE

Genocide is one of the most complicated human behaviors to comprehend from a psychological perspective, as it is the most heinous and abhorrent unleashing of a collective's otherwise hidden, dark, and disturbing drives of aggression and rage. It obliterates the difference between good and evil morally, between normal and abnormal psychologically. Morally, it leaves people unable to feel empathy and, hence, understand the ethical consequences and implications of their actions. This moral ineptitude allows people to act sadistically, even inhumanly, when they would otherwise never behave that way. The psychological state of primal pack mentality generates a sense of belonging, security, and social status among a group of people, justifying and normalizing the atrocities and genocide they inflict upon others. This group dynamic absolves perpetrators of their personal and moral responsibility, giving them a sense of higher purpose for the greater good of their "pack."

The psychological motivation for genocide is driven by emotions of fear, anger, and hatred. It is the result of long-term psychosocial and moral desensitization through propaganda and brainwashing, which diminishes and ultimately eliminates the perceived value of the stated enemy's human life. Genocide provides the opportunity for a person or group to direct their ingrained and mostly unconscious aggression towards the targeted other, whom they vilify, fear, and hate. For the aggressor, the targeted group's human existence has no more value than that of an animal or a plant to be controlled and eradicated.

Genocide does not happen overnight. Before any genocide begins, there is a long preparation period. In this period, the targeted race, people, ethnic group, or religious community is gradually reduced—in the eyes of the populace—to the level of something disgusting, something people find instantly abhorrent. The Nazis depicted the Jews as rats, while the Hutu described the Tutsi as cockroaches. Humans generally not only dislike rats and cockroaches, they seek to eliminate them from their natural habitat. Underpinning these metaphors is a hidden message, which the perpetrators use to subtly create an image of a grave threat to their existence. This image is both repulsive and dangerous. It further ignites people's defense mechanisms using fear and creates an urgent desire to eradicate the threat.

This imagery transforms the humanness of the targeted group into a kind of animalism, crude and vicious, to be despised and ultimately annihilated. The transformation becomes so deeply ingrained in the minds of the targeting group that their leaders can easily conjure into reality the most primordial aggression, itself animalism, to be unleashed on these "animals" they fear. The masses of the targeting group are effectively indoctrinated, manipulated into believing that the elimination of these "animals disguised as human beings" is a political imperative that is critical for their own survival. It is a sacred duty to be enacted immediately, and they will never be safe until they are successful. There is a potent urgency for mass murder when eliminating the targeted groups becomes a moral imperative, justifiable in itself.

The crucial point here is that, in most cases in human history, the targeting group's leaders have successfully convinced them that they are eliminating not human beings, but animals. This conviction allows the perpetrators to act under an illusion, freeing them from any guilty conscience. Not only do they fail to see their action as a heinous crime, but they view it as a heroic mission to accomplish. Psychologically numbed and morally insensitive to their own actions, the targeting group members are whipped into a frenzy to commit a collective crime without fully realizing the consequences of what they are doing.

Applying this concept to the Uyghur genocide, the image of Uyghurs as a virus is perfectly minimalistic and negative, portraying them as something malicious, dangerous, and critically contagious. This propaganda creates a simple, unforgettable image of Uyghurs, ensuring Han Chinese feel no sympathy for them. The psychological power of this constant propaganda should not be underestimated; it has made genocide psychologically permissible. The CCP's use of viral imagery has induced Han Chinese to participate in the execution of this massacre and to view it, not as a crime, but as a cultural cleansing. They have come to view it as a necessary task, the completion of which provides them with a sense of cleanliness or purification. It is nothing but ideological, social, and psychological hygiene. They are praised by their leaders and, more importantly, find their efforts self-rewarding.

Han Chinese find great satisfaction in making their life free of viruses, enemies, and moral vices, and implementing the Four Breaks will give them the same sense of achievement and safety. With the imagery used in the Four

Breaks, Uyghurs are viewed as a poisonous plant, rooted in the soil of their homeland. They must either be broken to the point where they will wither away completely, or they must be uprooted so that they and their descendants will never be able to grow on that land again.

Both viruses and roots are biological terms. By using these terms, the CCP projects an image of what a healthy social life for Han Chinese looks like and what the natural enemy of this organic life might be. A healthy life is what all human beings dream of as one of the key requirements for happiness, while organic life signifies harmony, growth, and prosperity. To be a force in opposition to this life is neither acceptable nor tolerated, as the law of nature dictates. It demands this healthy and organic lifestyle to be maintained and, when necessary, protected at all costs. The biological portrayal of their enemy calls for a natural, basic response. And so, it seems like common sense to eradicate this virus by destroying the evil roots of its dangerous ideologies. Uyghurs must be eradicated, as they will have no place in this biologically purified field.

This process can also be analyzed linguistically. To understand Chinese language as it relates to the psychology of their culture, we must look at it from a structuralist perspective. Han Chinese have a cognitive habit of understanding the world through images. For them, the world does not exist, primordially, as a conceptual whole. Rather, the world is encoded in small images as expressed in the character structure of their words, each of which signifies discrete concepts within a larger framework. In Chinese, the interactive formation of overall meaning occurs through the combination of parts in a particular structure, while the parts themselves are only meaningful by virtue of their interactions within the whole. When this language is used to describe Uyghurs in a simple, metaphorical way, Han Chinese accept these images quite easily. This format capitalizes upon their elemental cognitive habits to ensure they quickly grasp it, memorize it, and act on it. In this way, the urge for violence against Uyghurs has become entrenched in the psyche of Han Chinese in a biologically implicated, linguistically accepted, psychologically convenient, and politically compelling way.

Hitler used social Darwinism to provide a theoretical, pseudo-rational platform for his argument to justify the elimination of the Jews. Of course, social Darwinism was not responsible for Hitler forming the idea of the Jewish Holocaust. Hitler simply used it as a "logical" tool to convince the Germans, who are famous for rational thinking, that they were under threat of annihilation from a Jewish world conspiracy. In a similar vein, Xi Jinping is hijacking these biological terms and linguistic building blocks to make his murderous plan to eliminate Uyghurs sound natural to Chinese society. The metaphors supported by these terms appeal to the basic instincts of all Han Chinese for self-protection. Their life is under threat by a dangerous virus; therefore, they must defend against it. Using this tactic, the CCP can make

murder normative and pseudo-rational as they transform the inherently critical and independent thinking of Han Chinese into something deeply disturbed and disturbingly warped.

MORAL CONSIDERATIONS OF GENOCIDE — A CHINESE PERSPECTIVE

In Chinese philosophy, the concept of human nature is one of the central
themes. In *The Analects*, Confucius says that he considers a person's nature
to be innately good. He writes, "Man is born with uprightness. If one loses it,
he will be lucky if he escapes with his life."[1] Mencius, as a true successor to
Confucius, describes it more explicitly and writes, "If you let people follow
their feelings (original nature), they will be able to do good. This is what is
meant by saying that human nature is good. If a man does evil, it is not the
fault of his natural endowment."[2]

Diametrically opposite to Mencius, Hsün Tzu asserts, "The nature of man
is evil; his goodness is the result of his activity. Now, man's inborn nature is
to seek for gain . . . Now the nature of man is evil. It must depend on teachers
and laws to become correct and achieve propriety and righteousness and then
it becomes disciplined."[3] Hsün Tzu's view of human nature is worth considering. In a critical argument against Mencius, he stipulates that if human
beings were inherently good, then they would not need rituals regulating
social harmony or require sages to create them. As the human heart is full of
envy and hatred, humans intrinsically have no morality, and rituals are created to train them to be good. However, believing in the essential perfectibility
of everyone, he maintains there is still some hope for corrigible human nature
by overcoming the demands of our desires.

Although they are fundamentally paradoxical, if we apply both theories to
the genocide of Uyghurs, we may uncover a different ethical perspective.
Where Confucius and Mencius fail to explain evil committed for the sake of
wicked pleasure, Hsün Tzu's philosophy fails to comprehend altruism and
the role of the rituals which aim to improve human interaction and harmony.
Neither of them addresses how social milieu and rules may shape human
nature, despite its intrinsic goodness or evilness, and how the same social
environment can make some human beings bad and others good if they are,
to a large extent, primordially determined. Given these contradictions, what
would be their respective perceptions regarding the human propensity for a
horrendous crime like genocide?

Hsün Tzu's theory is still relevant here. When intrinsic feelings of envy
and hatred divert a person from learned and correct pathways, they are simply reverting to their natural state of evilness, as a human is essentially a
fallen creature. Proper education, teaching, and discipline can alter a person's

path, but they will never be completely virtuous. While a man's actions can be corrected, he remains intrinsically evil. One might say that man's true nature is contained or containable.

We can easily see this philosophical outlook at work in a CCP re-education center. Authorities and guards are already conditioned to think Uyghurs are innately evil and morally blind by nature. They can be improved, as it is always possible for one to reform oneself, although this result is not guaranteed. Pessimistically, Hsün Tzu is skeptical of people's capacity to achieve this transformation; however, this does not mean that, in principle, it is impossible for them to change.

In the eyes of communist educators, the reformation of individuals can occur by force, which is not what Hsün Tzu endorses. The presupposition that human beings are inherently evil is central to the communists' position, and they see enforced education as the key to reformation. By disciplining them and delivering them from mistakes and hatred, the communists allow previously wayward citizens to live a socially and politically acceptable life. However, according to Hsün Tzu, their efforts will be in vain, as humans are fundamentally incorrigible. Continuous discipline will be indispensable to maintain control of human desires, which have the potential for developing into something dangerous and evil. As they strive to reach their stated goal, the communists are not afraid to resort to equally evil behavior. For them, the end certainly justifies the means, so one must employ whatever means, force, or torture are necessary, be they equally or even more evil than the imagined enemy. This concept is understood in Chinese wisdom as "fighting evil with evil" (以毒攻毒).

Using this method, the communists can detach themselves from any kind of moral reasoning. To engage in genuine moral reasoning, one generally begins by reflecting on the significance of an end as opposed to a means. Moral reasoning refers to a cognitive process that individuals use to determine if the method is justified by the result, examining the difference between right and wrong by using logic and practical reason. It is a mental process that involves weighing the possible consequences (ends) of each given action (means).

For communists, the goal of eliminating viruses in human minds through discipline and education is for the greater good; therefore, their actions in achieving it are intrinsically justifiable. This preconceived certainty prevents them from questioning their own methods. They have themselves already been brainwashed to brainwash others and have lost the capacity to reflect on the ethics of their actions. They believe they are dealing with the primitive minds of barbarians in a natural state. Therefore, there is no need to consider the civility of the means. Such primitive people must be changed by force from their natural condition, crooked and self-ignorant as they are. They deserve the method their nature requires.

IMPLICATIONS OF GENOCIDE FROM THE
STANFORD PRISON EXPERIMENT

Moving beyond the essentialist views of human nature and putting aside the notion of humans as intrinsically good or bad, we need to take into account two crucial factors: the impact of a social environment and the role of free will. The Stanford prison experiment is an excellent demonstration of how a controlled environment can seemingly change a good person into a bad guard, regardless of what nature that person possesses in advance. The results of the experiment are quite shocking, revealing how an ordinary person, given a position of power, could show extreme cruelty to people under their control. Although this experiment quickly became controversial in the academic world, there are still significant lessons in it to be learned for our purposes.

We should note, initially, that the guards in this scenario showed no interest in who the prisoners were and what crimes they had committed. Instead, they were each solely focused on their own position as a guard and their responsibility for keeping the prisoners subordinate through discipline. They showed no capacity to self-reflect on their intensifying disciplinary measures or to consider the effects on inmates, who were innocent actors in the role. One participant, Dave Eshleman, who acted in the experiment as a lead prison guard, told the BBC later, soberly: "After the first day I noticed nothing was happening. It was a bit of a bore, so I made the decision I would take on the persona of a very cruel prison guard."

At the same time, prisoners, who were referred to only by their numbers and treated harshly, rebelled and blockaded themselves inside their cells. The guards saw this as a challenge to their authority, so they broke up the demonstration and began to impose their will. The head experimenter Professor Zimbardo describes it like this: "Suddenly, the whole dynamic changed as they believed they were dealing with dangerous prisoners, and at that point it was no longer an experiment."[4]

There are three crucial points to note here. Firstly, those in the designated role of prison guard had no preconditioning or brainwashing. Guards in this scenario had the situational opportunity and personal capacity to choose a point on the moral and ethical spectrum between good and evil. Either they could be a good guard, exercising their rational capacity to consider the nature, scope, and consequences of their actions, or they could be a bad guard.

Secondly, both parties are locked in a situation with a set of power dynamics. The guards understand that they have both responsibility and authority to maintain order inside the prison. They cannot allow this authority to be challenged in any way, as it is the basis for their legitimacy. The prisoners are naturally in a subordinate position and must obey the rules of the prison as presented to them through the authority of the guards. The "us vs. them" dynamic is established quickly and encourages guards to exert their power to quell all acts of disobedience swiftly to reinforce their legitimacy. The source of this legitimacy is their prescribed authority, and the authority cannot be challenged, lest it undermine their legitimacy.

Thirdly, a turning point occurs when guards begin to believe that the prisoners are dangerous, as the experimenter, Professor Zimbardo, observes. This conviction makes the guards more determined, and it encourages them to act without spending much time considering the consequences of their actions. This moment of belief is when the guards enter a morally neutral blind zone. They believe their actions are necessary to avert danger; therefore, their actions are perfectly justifiable.

If we apply the lessons of this psychological experiment to guards in China's concentration camps, we can see several parallels. While they, too, are free to choose being a good guard over being a bad guard, they are already brainwashed to believe that they are dealing with socially dangerous inmates infected with fatal viruses. Given this context, the behavior of the camp guards is far more worrisome. They rarely think independently, critically, or ethically about what they are doing to inmates, much like guards in the Stanford experiment. They are, to some extent, psychologically and morally blind to the atrocities they are committing. In reality, while they may differentiate themselves entirely from inmates, over whom they have full control, both guards as perpetrators of cruelty and the inmates as victims of their cruelty are ultimately victims of the same impersonal, immoral, and criminal system. The only significant distinction to be made is that guards still possess the cognitive capacity, however limited, to question. They have the theoretical ability to examine what is happening inside the camps, including their own behavior. With some physical and cognitive distance from the camps, they have an opportunity to look at things from a different perspective.

However, all guards are trained to reject the evidence of their eyes or simply to hide it from the public. As George Orwell said, "the party told you to reject the evidence of your eyes and ears. It was their final, most essential command."[5] The command of the CCP is absolute, and the guards, who execute its command, do so as if they have seen and heard nothing. There is little to no chance that they will be open to consciously receiving and critically analyzing evidence about the life they are taking control of within the walls of the camps. Another reason for absolute concealment of life inside the camps is that the CCP is extremely secretive and, therefore, maintains strict control over information management. There is simply no tolerance for any leakage of information.

One can assume certainly that at least some guards, insiders, and officials managing the camps are fully loyal to the CCP and not inclined to question its mistreatment of Uyghurs and other inmates. They enjoy displaying their racial and authoritative superiority to inmates through humiliation, torture, and brainwashing practices, physically, emotionally, and sexually. While inflicting unbearable pain, they are delighted to see inmates crawling in front of them as slaves, begging for mercy, and making promises of cooperation. It is a moment of great exultation when their position as masters from the Middle Kingdom, the cradle of one of the most ancient civilizations, is reasserted. Inmates are required to assume two simultaneous roles together—to be a passive receiver of the guards' mastery and to be a helpless witness to their enormous power, exerted through torture. For those in authority, inmates are like a mirror that reflects their absolute authority. They revel in their position as somebody who decides who will live and who will die. Still, they must struggle with contradictory impulses. Hence, for them, to kill an inmate is a contradictory thing, as it fulfills the ultimate purpose of the whole operation but abruptly ends the enjoyment of their unrestricted power.

WHO IS RESPONSIBLE FOR THE UYGHUR GENOCIDE?

As the CCP is fully aware, as long as the world lacks substantiated evidence about the camps, they can continue to eliminate Uyghurs in secret. Nobody knows what will happen once all Uyghurs inside the camps, and those in the prisons, to which many camp inmates have secretly been relocated, have perished. At that point, it will be too late for the international community to bring the CCP to justice for the Uyghurs victims. There may perhaps be no Uyghurs left to feel relieved that justice is finally served, and moral compensation is paid.

The immensity of this crime the CCP is committing compels them to keep it under a cloak of darkness. Documents that first revealed the *modus operandi* of a vast chain of Chinese concentration camps were leaked in November 2019 and showed that to "allow any escapes" was strictly prohibited.[6] The documents describe "preventing escape" as a top priority. The order demands round-the-clock video surveillance "with no blind spots" to monitor every moment of an inmate's day. Control of every aspect of their lives is so comprehensive that they must be assigned a specific place in dormitories and classrooms, even in the lunchtime queue.

This chilling description shows how the secrecy of life inside the camps is maintained. It also tells us how Uyghurs and other inmates are ruthlessly monitored so as not to reveal to the world what unbearable torture they are going through. This priority stands at odds with how the CCP presents China diplomatically to the international community—inviting them to "visit Xinjiang" to see things on the ground. If the CCP is confident in what it is doing, in the accomplishment of thought transformations of inmates through a series of brainwashing operations inside the camps, why is it so afraid of escapes?

Communist masters are mindful of the consequences a revelation of this crime to the outside world would have. The vehement denial of the CCP over its practice inside the camps is deeply disturbing. It is not simply that they are lying or not being transparent about what they are doing, but they are concealing one of the most hideous crimes in the twenty-first century. It is not only the CCP who works to hide the truth, but all the Chinese officials who have been involved in this crime. All are equally concealing it from the world for fear of being blamed for it. The state machine and the people working for it are united in their efforts to escape responsibility for this crime. They are acting together to avoid any revelations, as they have acted together to be complicit in committing this crime.

The guards must be aware that what they are doing to other human beings could never be done publicly but is only possible in a state-sanctioned secretive environment. For them, whether or not their action is legal is irrelevant. They only know that they are doing what they are told to do. In the future, if they are questioned by an international or national court about their crimes, they could answer the same way the Nazi, Adolf Eichmann, did. Eichmann was a high-ranking SS officer who was tasked with managing the logistics of mass deportation of Jewish people to ghettos and extermination camps in Nazi-occupied Eastern Europe during WWII. In defending himself at his trial in Jerusalem in 1961, he stated, "My heart was light and joyful in my work, because the decisions were not mine."[7] He concluded, "To sum it all up, I must say that I regret nothing."

What would a Chinese Adolf Eichmann say at some future hypothetical international court, in their own defense, against charges of complicity in carrying out genocide against Uyghurs in the camps? Would they put all blame on Xi Jinping, saying that he is the mastermind behind this horrendous crime and that they were a tool devoid of free will in executing it? They may repeat that they only did what they were asked to do. Will Han Chinese experience collective guilt at the end of this genocide, as Carl Gustav Jung theorized? How much "free will" is sufficient for a person under a repressive regime to take responsibility for their involvement in genocide? How much should the CCP, as a political institution, be subject to moral condemnation after this genocide is finished? What will be the responsibility of the members of CCP for this crime? Will this genocide ever finally be over, so that Uyghurs can say, "Never Again," echoing the desperate outcry of the Jewish people after WWII?

Despite the fact they are not the decision-makers who initially conspired to torture and eliminate Uyghurs, the perpetrators of this genocide are still in a position to decide how to implement it, to some extent. Hence, it is not morally justifiable that they have simply done what they were asked. It is true that they have been deceived into believing they are at war with enemies of the state, the "abnormal" addition to their society. Therefore, they expect their actions to bring about social good, not moral disaster. We can assume they might defend themselves in some future court by stating these beliefs: "What we were doing was for the greater good of society. We acted in self-defense against potential terrorists who would have destroyed us, had we not destroyed them first." Perhaps their actions are understandable in the context of self-defense. In this context, the ethics of survival seems far greater and more important than human rights. The only issue here is that their survivalist mentality has been activated against an imaginary enemy, one that only exists in their minds.

The perception that there is a biological threat carried by every Uyghur lessens the weight of any guilt the guards may feel. They see themselves as inflicting a necessary evil upon Uyghurs and others, inside and outside the camps. They are dealing with a social disease, like a doctor responding to a viral epidemic. Just as a doctor is not questioned for their heavy-handed quarantining measures and methods, their eradication of Uyghurs is also not questioned. However, the serious question is this: Can they deny what they did criminally? No. They willingly applied for the role and worked wholeheartedly for an evil scheme to exterminate innocent people. Whatever their convictions, they must know that taking someone's organs against their will is a crime, for they would not allow their own organs to be taken without permission this way. They must know that to rape another person is a crime, for, at least, they would protest if they were forced to endure it this way. They must know that to inflict torture upon others is a crime, for certainly they would not wish to be tortured by others this way. Clearly, even though China continues to present this genocide as a voluntary re-education process, nobody—including the mouthpiece of the CCP—would willingly be subjected to this process themselves.

We have now discussed the psychological, ethical, and moral culpability of the Han Chinese in general, and the camp guards in particular for their actions in this genocide. What about the CCP? What shall we say about the CCP's responsibility, as a ruling party, for this situation? The CCP is one of the most dangerous political organizations in human history, having propagated this genocide using cutting-edge technologies with unprecedented levels of cruelty.

Unlike most previous and contemporary totalitarian states, China has enormous capacity and resources to support ongoing, organic evolution. It is, in essence, a kind of organic totalitarianism. The regime functions by absorbing new ideas, technologies, financial opportunities, and cultural commodities while expanding its influence and control in an astonishingly insidious way. It has two critical components: aggressive absorption and non-confrontational expansionism. This process can be likened to the fundamental function of an organism, the simplest metaphor being a seed. The seed uses its own vital biological potential but also takes in anything external that is beneficial for its growth, including sunlight, soil, water, and chemicals. It does this to expand both underground by deepening its roots and above ground by spreading its body outward. The seed is flexible while realizing its own deterministic potential to promote strong, unlimited, and sustainable growth.

The CCP has successfully acted in this same organic way, with an ultimate aim that does not include consideration of benefiting anybody but themselves. For example, it is not bound by its own ideology, as other totalitarian states generally are. It aligns itself on the surface with any state or ideology from which it can benefit. Unlike notorious totalitarian regimes like the Nazis and North Korea, China has an excellent business relationship with the key Western countries and institutions, including the United States, UK, and EU. This level of flexibility implies that everything is possible, as long as rapid growth remains the priority. However, it is impossible to change the inner biological code, the fundamental existence and function of the CCP. They can adopt as many key aspects of capitalism as possible: a free market, sophisticated financial management, and advanced educational frameworks, and so on. However, the market can only be free as long as it serves the interests of the CCP members first. Financial sectors must be regulated in order to develop the national economy while maintaining social stability. Education is, first and foremost, an area for ideological upbringing of new generations as successors to the CCP. In short, all changes in China are possible on condition that absolute rule of the CCP over everything remains unchallenged and stable.

Within this context, the CCP carries out the Uyghur genocide by creating an organic threat as an imperative for public safety. It also functions in accordance with biological principles in a larger sense, as its existence depends on a parasitic reliance on external benefits as well as stringent internal controls that mandate self-preservation. The external benefits are safeguarded through a vast network of overseas espionage that infiltrates the business sectors, military institutions, universities, and research centers of almost all key Western countries. The internal controls are safeguarded through a thought-control process, which they apply to everyone in China.

Even with a cursory examination, the CCP emerges as an evil institution, obliterating the fundamental differences between the individual and the collective. In particular, the Uyghur genocide has mobilized Chinese society to act as one to fight against Uyghurs as "terrorists." No Uyghur is immune to this sweeping categorization, resulting in collective punishment. In the Uyghur genocide, as in any other genocide, no individuality is taken into account; instead, all are subsumed into an imagined collective that is hated, vilified, and targeted for obliteration. If the CCP is targeting Uyghurs collectively with this genocide, should there be any difference between individual responsibility and collective responsibility?

Generally, we assume that each person is responsible for the consequences of their actions, as these are a product of his will and decisions, and no other person can share this responsibility, unless they have acted together. There is another level of responsibility stemming from one's involvement in actions conducted by a collective or an institution. Members of a group must take on collective responsibility at varying degrees, depending on the level of their involvement. When group members act, they act using their own will, although the leaders of the group may have already determined the parameters, methods, and goals of their actions. In this pre-determined context, there remains room for individuals to act deliberately and willfully to promote the interest of the group, and to take full responsibility for their actions individually.

In considering the complexity of human attitude, behavior, and values before and during a genocide, it is clear that morality and psychology are at work extensively in the background. It is not merely that human beings are inherently evil enough to commit genocide. Morality, as defined by principles, values, desires, and practices that maintain or promote human welfare, may be psychologically influenced, and even altered by external forces. Some of these influences enabling genocide include toxic social milieu, manipulative leadership, or dangerous ideologies, which may affect people's psychological morality and hence their behavior. As people respond to these forces, they may engage in profoundly immoral actions never critically questioning the moral value of their thoughts, feelings, and actions, let alone the consequences. It is crucial to note that this altered psychology, influenced by external forces, can subvert existing moral principles and emotions. Therefore, we need not be intrinsically evil to become *génocidaires* in a deterministic sense. It merely requires a guidable, if not necessarily gullible, mind to be programmed to believe that survival depends on the annihilation of another group of people. In this way, genocide is pre-justified.

If a genocidal intent is deterministic, something that we have inherently and over which we have no absolute control, then it is still difficult to ascribe individual moral responsibility to the perpetrators. This deterministic outlook will ultimately downplay the severity of participation in the most horrific crimes by excluding the role of free choice, pardoning the immorality of genocide with the psychological excuse of determinism.

It must be stressed that genocidal intent and action are not deterministic, and they still require the free choice of individuals. If we ignore this point, we cannot condemn or punish anyone for their complicity in acts of genocide. Nor can we understand why not everybody in the same society participates in a sweeping act of genocide. This phenomenon tells us compellingly that there are still some people who have moral immunity against the sinister, hypnotizing ideologies of the fascists, ultra-nationalists, sociopaths, and dictators who unleash hatred upon others which may lead to committing genocide.

Genocide is not a criminal act of killing only one person; the intent is to annihilate a group of people. Genocide indiscriminately kills as many innocent people as possible until the absolute extinction of the targeted group is achieved. There is no statistical benchmark for us to define genocide by the number of people killed. However, any genocide requires the participation of many people to commit a crime against humanity together, even though an individual, like Hitler, or a small group, may initially provoke it. This collective action brings about colossal damage beyond imagination to the victims of genocide. This is precisely the aim of these provocateurs and perpetrators: to increase the level of catastrophic damage as much as possible, to leave no living soul alive, and to erase all traces of their existence. Their hatred is bottomless and boundless, and it triggers the release of the hidden and violent animality inside perpetrators towards their victims.

We all know that in such a collective act, individual participants feel morally protected, as they believe that they are carrying out a sacred duty at the direction of their superiors or leaders. As such, individual responsibility is numbed or nullified, as the individual is convinced internally and externally by their leaders that they are forever immune from the harsh judgments of history. However, while genocide kills many individual victims mercilessly, it is not able to kill individual conscience completely. Perpetrators are still able to make a moral choice with independent deliberation and decision, both during and after the genocide. Therefore, the responsibility for genocide is as much individual as collective. Further, the ultimate responsibility is individual as long as they are free to choose their participation in the genocidal act. Therefore, nothing can save individual perpetrators from the moral responsibility for their genocidal actions, regardless of who they are in the end.

To understand this point further, let us think about it through a social psychology perspective, using Le Bon's theory of the group mind. In a social psychological classic called *The Crowd: A Study of the Popular Mind*, Gustave Le Bon described the behavior of revolutionary mobs in the French revolution as indicative of what he called the group mind or collective unconscious. Shared by all men, even those who were civilized, this form of collective unconscious consolidates a drive towards one common goal. It provides participants of this collective consciousness with a veil of anonymity, allowing them to devolve from their civilized state into a position of "primitive people." As Le Bon put it, "by the very fact that he forms part of an organized group, a man descends several rungs down the ladder of civilization. Isolated, he may be a cultivated individual, in a crowd, he is a barbarian—that is, a creature acting by instinct."[8] The descent to this level opens up a Pandora's Box inside of an individual, as they yield to collective instincts that are dangerous, blind, and destructive. Had he been alone, he would have kept these under constraint. The protection of anonymity brings an ensuing loss of personal responsibility in a crowd, coupled with a form of contagion, where normally proscribed acts are then mimicked and re-enacted.

Though it is true that a man tends to be led to acts that are impulsive, irritable, changeable, and driven by unconsciousness, it is still arguable that rational thinking is not totally absent in the commission of such a horrendous action. Rationality permeates everything in any society in the form of "social rationality," shaping our conscious and unconscious minds. Under the spell of this social rationality regulating the appropriateness of an end to a means in any social activity, a man cannot free himself completely from the social commandment that murder is not acceptable, which is the basis of established social customs, taboos, rituals, principles, and manners. Moreover, his conscious mind has been built within this prohibitive rule since his childhood, as psychoanalysis teaches us. While it is possible to neglect this commandment amid the frenzies of a genocidal act in the crowds, thoughts of the criminality of killing a human being are never easy to switch off, unless one is mentally disturbed, unstable, or ill. These thoughts are operative deep in our subconscious mind as a universal principle legitimized by all religions, laws, theories, and practices. Each person has been instilled innately with this principle, however viciously and murderously he acts. It may exist differently in one's mind while committing a murder—one has no desire to be killed and may be killing to prevent being killed by others. The imperative of not being killed is the inverse principle of not killing anyone else.

A crowd does provide an opportunity for an individual to remain anonymous, absolving themselves of responsibility for their actions. However, it is interesting to note that there is a paradox in acting in crowds—in the course of collective violence, the most private, innermost instincts are released. Stated otherwise, the more collectivized the action is, the more personalized the release of instincts, drives, and urges is. As such, a man does not fully disappear into the collective. Instead, he releases his deep-seated individualistic insecurities to express himself freely in his own most primitive way. Hence, as he expresses himself in freedom, he is fully responsible for his individual actions in the strictest sense of the word, paradoxically, within the collectivized crowd situation.

To commit a crime within a crowd gives perpetrators an illusion that an action enacted by everybody is an action carried out by nobody, in the end. An action can be justifiably repeated as long as everybody is doing it. This perception eats away at personal responsibility when actors believe they are as much acquitted of any wrongdoing as their peers. However, what still remains in such a situation is the possibility for everybody to act in a way that upholds intrinsic morals and principals; it is sufficient to say they were free to choose the nature and style of their action in the first place. Moreover, others were also free to imitate other's action. Hence, all are free in the end; therefore, all are responsible. There is a collective responsibility, which does not absolve individual responsibility, and which cannot be evaded or delegated to others.

The question is, who will ultimately be responsible for the Uyghur genocide: Xi Jinping, the CCP, or any individual directly involved in the extermination of Uyghurs? First, from an individual responsibility perspective, anyone who has taken part in the Uyghur genocide is strictly responsible for their actions. Ultimately, the highest responsibility can be attributed to Xi Jinping as the chief architect of this horrendous crime, as opposed to an ordinary person who supports it. Accountability must be ascribed to individuals proportionately, depending on the level of their participation, the role they played and the options that they choose. As genocide can also be the result of collective genocidal intent, the CCP—being a collective membership system—must also be responsible for it. The CCP has committed foreseeable harm to Uyghurs through its regular and coordinated operations, without any legal basis or moral justification. Logically, it follows that all members of the CCP, as well as those outside of it who were involved in this crime against humanity, should be held accountable in any future possible litigation.

NOTES

1. Confucius, *"The Analects,"* in *A Source Book in Chinese Philosophy*, ed. Wing-Tsit Chan (Princeton, NJ: Princeton University Press, 1973), 29.

2. Mencius, "The Book of Mencius," in Chan, *A Source Book*, 52.

3. Hsün Tze, "The Book of Hsün Tze," in Chan, *A Source Book*, 28.

4. Alastair Leithead, "Stanford Prison Experiment Continues to Shock," BBC News, August 17, 2011, https://www.bbc.com/news/world-us-canada-14564182.

5. George Orwell, *Animal Farm and 1984* (Boston: Harcourt Books, 2003), 162.

6. Emma Graham-Harrison and Juliette Garside, "'Allow No Escapes': Leak Exposes Reality of China's Vast Prison Camp Network," *The Guardian*, Guardian News and Media, November 24, 2019, https://www.theguardian.com/world/2019/nov/24/china-cables-leak-no-escapes-reality-china-uighur-prison-camp.

7. Alan Rosenthal, "Eichmann, Revisited," *The Jerusalem Post*, April 20, 2011, https://www.jpost.com/Jerusalem-Report/Jewish-World/Eichmann-Revisited.

8. Gustave Le Bon, *The Crowd: A Study of The Popular Mind*, (Auckland: The Floating Press, 2009), 33.

Chapter Eight

World as a Bystander

Brenton Tarrant is a twenty-eight-year-old Australian white supremacist who was responsible for the massacre of Muslim worshippers at two New Zealand mosques on March 15, 2019. He stated in his manifesto that "the nation with the closest political and social values" to his own was China, adding that he admired "non-diverse" nations. His perspective was as much a shock to me as his abhorrent crime. It was shocking in the sense that he identified himself with the ideologies and actions of the CCP, which is destroying everything signifying Uyghur identity. If he were in China, he might perhaps be a faithful guard in a concentration camp, where he could unleash his hatred towards Uyghurs and other Turkic Muslims in a sanctioned way. He would have the opportunity to instill terror in their dying minds to restore respect and fear. As Heinrich Himmler said, "The best political weapon is the weapon of terror. Cruelty commands respect. Men may hate us. But we don't ask for their love, only for their fear." Tarrant's hatred was so deeply rooted in the Machiavellian modern politics of love and fear that he was willing to align himself with any group or government, as long as they harbored as much animosity towards Muslims as he did.

The biggest irony of Tarrant's desire for ideological alignment with China is that while the CCP suppresses the victims of terrorism, it also harbors deep-seated antipathy to white supremacy. The Century of Humiliation (百年国耻), which is a foundational motivator of modern Chinese nationalism, is a reaction to white imperialism, colonialism, and supremacy. While Tarrant imagines the CCP cooperating with him in eliminating Muslims from its society, it is not as ethnically diversifiable as he believes. What he does not mention is that the CCP is purging other believers as well in an equally ruthless manner, including Christians, Buddhists, and Falun Gong practitioners, among others. If he intends to be ideologically supportive of the CCP's anti-Muslim stance, then he should also be politically supportive of its anti-religious position as a whole, while also embracing its historical anti-white-supremacy agenda.

OTHER MUSLIM NATIONS

Brenton Tarrant is not the only person who is supporting the CCP's genocide of Uyghurs because of their hatred towards Muslims. Ironically, many Muslim leaders have also expressed their solidarity with China in eliminating Uyghurs in the name of fighting against terrorism. Recently, thirty-seven countries, including Pakistan, Saudi Arabia, Algeria, Russia, and Cuba, sent a joint letter of support of the CCP's policies in East Turkistan (Xinjiang Uyghur Autonomous Region) to the UN, outnumbering the twenty-two Western countries who had previously sent a letter outlining concerns. [1]

Saudi Crown Prince Mohammed Bin Salman publicly supported the CCP's genocide of Uyghur Muslims, stating they have the right to undertake "anti-terrorism" and "de-extremism" measures. [2] Some other leaders are more diplomatic and nuanced enough to cover up their tacit support under the veil of "amnesia." Pakistani Prime Minister Imran Khan and Indonesian Prime Minister Joko Widodo dodged questions on the reported detention of as many as two million Muslims in East Turkistan, saying they "didn't know much" about the issue in an interview with the *Financial Times*. [3] With a blatant display of feigned ignorance, they turned their backs on Muslim Uyghurs for fear of a potential retaliatory financial backlash from China.

It must be noted that both Pakistan and Saudi Arabia are heavily dependent on China as a deterrent power to deal with their respective archenemies, India and Iran. While it supports these countries' political goals against their enemies, China can avail itself of their unfailing, unconditional, and timely support to win its domestic struggles against Uyghurs and other Turkic nationalities. In this win-win situation, other nations are turning a blind eye to the Uyghur crisis, while China ignores the Islamic identity of these countries, the same identity that is ruthlessly suppressed in the Uyghur motherland. This mutual support and protection are so entrenched that these countries raise no objection to China's razing of mosques and burning of the Qur'an, the holy book that is the foundation of their theocratic statehood. They do not even react to China labeling them as countries where Uyghurs are accused of being infected by their ideological viruses, the deadly viruses that could spread to others back home. These countries must tolerate the insults that China inflicts upon them, unlike other insults towards the Islamic faith, as China's money is their new religion.

Currently, almost all Islamic states are silent over the CCP's operation of the concentration camps, tacitly condoning genocide against Uyghurs who share their religion. These countries' governments have a similar style of governance and a history of suppressing democratic voices, like the CCP. Given this context, they can easily justify their silence as it serves a strategic purpose of solidarity with their suppression of their respective peoples. Like China, they can each portray themselves as victims of terrorism, using the excuse to defend the vital interests of their repressive regimes.

Few heads of the government, anywhere, have openly condemned inhuman treatment of Uyghurs under the draconian rule of the CCP in China. None of the Nobel Peace Laureates have ever called for China, even symbolically, to respect the fundamental human rights of Uyghurs. Even the Dalai Lama, himself a victim and occasional critic of this very same regime, has failed to speak out on this issue. Given the absence of significant and coordinated international condemnation, China is emboldened to broaden the scope of the concentration camps in the future.

WORLD ORGANIZATIONS

United Nations Secretary-General Antonio Guterres raised the plight of Uyghur Muslims in China's Xinjiang region during a visit to Beijing in April 2019. His approach could best be described as paying obligatory lip service to the crisis rather than seriously advocating at a higher level. Responding to the lack of worldwide efforts to put an end to the Uyghur crisis, Kelley Currie, head of the Office of Global Criminal Justice at the US State Department, said that "We would just like to see the UN stand up for its own values in this situation, take its human rights commitments seriously, and actually speak out to protect these vulnerable populations."[4] The UN's lack of serious commitment to this issue brings into question its validity as an organization with the capacity to prevent genocide, as is its stipulated role within the Geneva Convention. It reminds us of the gross failure of the UN under the leadership of Kofi Annan to prevent the Rwanda genocide in 1994, resulting in 800,000 deaths, or almost one-tenth of the country's population. The Rwanda genocide took place over approximately one hundred days and did not even spare those who sought sanctuary in churches and missions. An independent report compiled by Ingvar Carlsson, the former Swedish Prime Minister, stated that this episode "will forever be remembered as one of the most abhorrent events of the 20th century . . . The international community did not prevent the genocide, nor did it stop the killing once it had begun."[5]

These lessons were not heeded by the UN under the leadership of UN Secretary-General Antonio Guterres when it came to preventing the Rohingyas from falling prey to the state-sponsored genocide perpetrated by the Burmese regime. While Antonio Guterres raised this crisis with many countries, the result was ultimately the same: the Burmese government has not stopped the genocide, nor has it acknowledged that it committed one of the most horrendous crimes against humanity. In the unfolding of this horrific genocide, we saw not only the impotence of the UN and inaction of many Western countries, but also the voracious defense of the atrocities by the once-beloved human rights champion elected to save them: Aung San Suu Kyi.

Once venerated as the role model for human rights fighters all around the world, Aung San Suu Kyi has now shown her despicable anti-Islamic face throughout these events without the slightest remorse. She is as horrible a perpetrator now as the Burmese regime that she had criticized before. There remains no critical difference between her position and the position of the Burmese regime on this genocide, the regime against which she fought so bravely before rising to power. There is a vast moral difference between the old Aung San Suu Kyi, a human rights fighter, and the new Aung San Suu Kyi, a human rights violator in her role as the first State Counsellor of Burma. Ironically, she once said, "It is not power that corrupts but fear. Fear of losing power corrupts those who wield it and fear of the scourge of power corrupts those who are subject to it. . . ."[6] Her stance on the Rohingya genocide proves the opposite of what she meant in this quote—it is not the fear, but the power that she previously fought against that corrupted her, not only politically but also morally. If it is fear that has changed her, then it is the fear of losing this same power that she had initially vied for in the name of fighting for democracy in Burma.

In this crisis, we have learned two things. Firstly, power still commands the most prestige for those deceptive, so-called power-haters, liberal thinkers, or freedom fighters. Secondly, inaction is still the default response of the international community, acting as a bystander despite well-documented evidence about this genocide rather than as an actor to bring about its end. The first lesson painfully reveals that power can still corrupt "angels" whose hearts are fueled by hatred for those worshipping the wrong god. The second lesson is that the international community, including the United Nations, has not learned the lessons of previous genocides, like the Holocaust, Cambodian, Rwandan, and Rohingya genocides.

While he has paid more attention to the Rohingya genocide, Antonio Guterres has limited himself to mentioning the Uyghur crisis only a couple of times. This inattention comes even though it was the UN that revealed there was credible information showing China is holding a million Uyghurs in "counter-extremism centers." If the fact that China is incarcerating this number of human beings in camps is of any significance to the UN, Guterres should address it seriously. The same organization that has been quick to criticize small and weak countries in Africa, Latin America, or Asia for human rights violations has shown its own weakness, hypocrisy, smallness and insignificance when it comes to criticizing a real bully, the world's second-largest superpower. In keeping its silence on the Uyghur genocide, the UN has acted as a bystander at best and as a bully at worst. For there is no difference between the perpetrator of a genocide and the silent witness to it, as they are both ultimately supporting the same result.

The UN is a global organization aimed at facilitating and overcoming common challenges faced by humanity in the spirit of shared responsibility. However, it appears the UN is unable to prevent or intervene in crimes against humanity. This impotence begs the following question: How could the UN still be representing humanity's vital interests? I can only propose some possible reasons for the UN's inability to act effectively to end this and other crimes against humanity. Perhaps, the problem is caused by its structural deficiency or by its inherent incapacity to diffuse the manipulations of countries that abuse its principles. A particular Member State, China, may also be so overpowering that it prevents the action on the UN's moral and likely legal obligation to intervene to combat this genocide. Maybe the UN is actually a mosaic organization, only embodying the endless conflicts of values and interests of individual Member States, without ever providing a solution. Whatever the reason, the UN is failing to fulfill its *raison d'être*.

DRAWING GLOBAL ATTENTION TO THE UYGHUR GENOCIDE

Some scholars around the world are working hard to highlight the Uyghur crisis, under the leadership of Professor Sean Roberts of George Washington University, with a public online campaign called "Statement by concerned scholars on China's mass detention of Turkic minorities."[7] This statement is crucial, as it sheds light on the aim, scope, and methods of the mass internment of Uyghurs, Kazakhs, and others in the concentration camps. More importantly, it concludes with several action points to end these atrocities. More than seven hundred scholars, mostly from the West, have signed the statement to express their concerns over one of the most egregious human rights violations this world has seen.

The only country placing moral, if primarily diplomatic, pressure on China to end its egregious practice of eliminating the cultural and religious identity of Uyghurs, Kazakhs, and others, is the United States of America (US). While US President Donald Trump has remained silent over this crisis, other US politicians including Senator Marco Rubio, Congressman Christopher Smith, and US Secretary of State Mike Pompeo, among others, have kept this crisis high on the US agenda. In March 2019, a bipartisan group of US lawmakers sent a letter to Mr. Pompeo, expressing their urgent concerns that "The administration has taken no meaningful action in response to the situation in Xinjiang."[8] On 27 May 2020, the US House of Representatives passed the Uyghur Human Rights Policy Act of 2020, in recognition of the rapid deterioration of the human rights of Uyghurs and other Turkic Muslims.[9] The bill is calling for sanctions against officials in China responsible for human rights abuses in the country's western region of Xinjiang. The latest move to strengthen the US stance toward China came nearly two weeks after the Republican-controlled Senate approved the bill to put pressure on Beijing over the Uyghur issue, which was later signed into law by President Donald Trump.[10]

However, the diplomatic efforts of the US government to hold China to account have not proved adequate or effective. Arguably, all diplomatic efforts will likely fail and will be limited as they are attempting to negotiate with a dictator. At what point, once all other diplomatic avenues have been explored, is there a case for more affirmative action? Xi Jinping is quite happy with diplomatic efforts and negotiations, as they give him more time to complete the genocide. He does not intend to succumb to any diplomatic entreaties from the international community to end his genocidal mission. If he did, then he would be the first dictator to do so. In the case of the Holocaust, it was not diplomatic efforts that saved and liberated the Jewish people from the concentration camps. Actually, the Nazis were diplomatically successful to put enormous pressure on other countries to be turning a blind eye to what was horribly happening to the Jews. Ultimately, it was the defeat of the nation-state, Germany, that forced the Nazis to open the gates of those horrific camps to the Allied and Soviet troops. The inability to stop the Rohingya genocide is another example that shows the ineffectiveness of diplomacy. This genocide is ongoing and will continue as long as the current Burmese regime responsible for it remains in power and is not challenged to stop its crimes against humanity.

All of these observations can only lead us to one likely, ultimate result. If there is little to no chance that a diplomatic effort can stop the CCP from committing crimes against humanity, and the world allows China's economically successful dictatorship to become the leading world power, then no one will ever have the courage or the resources to address this issue seriously. This scenario will result in the extinction of Uyghurs, one way or another. Therefore, while peaceful and diplomatic efforts are still indispensable in the effort to hold the perpetrators of genocide accountable, more decisive action is urgently needed. The result of the trade war unfolding between the US and China is significant, for example, as it may weaken the economic leverage China can wield over other countries as it threatens them to keep silent over its dangerous, genocidal ambitions. If this effort is unsuccessful, the future is terribly gloomy for Uyghurs.

REASONS FOR THE SILENCE

I should note here that the world still lacks a full understanding of what exactly is happening inside the concentration camps. The world became aware of the full scale of the Nazi concentration camps only after the camps were liberated. Photographs and first-person testimonies, both written and oral, exposed the horrific nature of the camps to people in other nations. However, in the case of the Uyghur genocide, the camps are not liberated yet, making it extremely difficult to get any evidence out. Unfortunately, as I mentioned at the beginning of this book, there is little to no leakage of information to the rest of the world about Uyghurs' mistreatment inside the camps. There are, however, a few victim statements given by Omir Bekali, Mihrigul Tursun, Gulbahar Jelilova, and Sairagul Sauytbay, among others, who detailed the horrific life inside CCP camps. All their testimonies describe the harrowing experiences they both had and bore witness to, disputing the official accounts of the camps offered by the CCP.

The CCP is not alone in its scheme to eliminate Uyghurs and other Turkic Muslims. It has recently been revealed that other well-known international organizations and scientists are assisting China in setting up suppressive facilities in East Turkistan. In February 2019, *New York Times* reported that China uses DNA information to track Uyghurs. Thermo Fisher, a Massachusetts company, and Dr. Kenneth Kidd, a prominent Yale University geneticist, coordinated to help China create a mega-system of surveillance and control. *The Independent* also reported that a security firm co-founded by former navy Seal and US military services contractor Erik Prince has been awarded a contract by the Chinese authorities to build a "training center" in the Xinjiang region.[11]

There is also information available, although it is limited and unverified, that suggests Chinese authorities are reaping great financial benefits by selling the organs of Uyghur inmates to domestic and international patients. As a result, the organ implantation business has been booming in China.[12] The convenience of organ availability means that there is enough supply down the line. Previously, it was the Falun Gong practitioners who were victims of organ harvesting. Now, Uyghurs and other Turkic inmates have been added to the list of unwilling donors who provide the supply of organs on-demand.

While some individuals and transnational corporations have assisted China with suppression mechanisms for financial benefit, the organs-for-profit operations inside camps reveal an even more alarming scenario. While the former speaks to the vulnerability of Uyghurs in murky international trade relationships, the latter indicates that Uyghurs can now be sold internationally as lucrative goods. Now, Uyghurs are being not just controlled and killed, but commoditized. In the ruthless business of organ harvesting seeking profits and benefits, many countries keep their lips tight on the silent deaths of Uyghurs.

Both these realities result in a deep sense of dehumanization, a horrific situation for Uyghurs in which they are not humans endowed with dignity and valued as an end-in-itself, as Kant would define it. Instead, they are reduced to something convenient and highly profitable. The commoditization of Uyghurs leaves them feeling insignificant, fetishized, and less than human. On a basic level, it reduces them to merely a body, one that is not only tortured to make them subservient to the command of their masters but is also sold for money if the need arises. This body retains the marks and memories of torture inflicted upon it by the communists. It has also become the physical space where the mind is attacked, emptied out, and conquered until it is incapable of any further resistance.

Another ordeal that Uyghurs are subject to is forced labor. Research publicized in news articles shows that some Uyghur inmates, after their release from the concentration camps, have been forced to work on production lines in factories. Here, they work long hours in an unhealthy and unsafe environment for minimum wages. The CCP builds new factories near or even within the camps, intending to increase labor efficiency via streamlined management, and importantly save on costs. The inmates have no choice other than to work against their will. This is a form of modern slave labor, praised by the CCP propagandists as "poverty alleviation."[13] Uyghur slave labor has a deceptive political propaganda purpose. It masks the true intention of the CCP to establish the vast number of concentration camps, allowing the CCP to justify the creation of them under the guise of "re-education centers," to train Uyghurs on necessary skills to be employed to alleviate their poverty.

Uyghur land in East Turkistan is famous for its cotton, 74 percent to 84 percent of China's cotton is grown there. This makes the region economically crucial for China, in its efforts to be the main exporter of textile products. However, Uyghur inmates or prisoners are the main labor force in all sections of the cotton supply chain, giving China an unfair competitive advantage in the global textile market through coercion and exploitation of Uyghur labor. This prison labor force has led the Uyghur Human Rights Project, a US-based group advocating for Uyghur rights in China, to describe the industry as a "cotton gulag."[14] Several global brands, such as H&M, Adidas, and Nike, are believed to have connections to East Turkistan's cotton, which none of them have yet confirmed. This is another example of how Uyghurs have become modern slaves—their bodies are commodities to make big money, and so is their labor. They have no right to their native land, bodily integrity, or their choice of profession. Instead, Uyghurs are either killed, mutilated, or left alive for the sole purpose of working as a slave. In short, they are alienated by force from their homes, bodies and from their labor—

from everything that sustains them as humans with dignity and a vision for the future.

To a significant degree, the world's silence is related to the CCP's justification that Uyghurs are terrorists, and Uyghurs in Syria fighting alongside ISIS are evidence that they pose a threat to national safety. Labelling Uyghurs as terrorists, either real or potential, because of their Islamic faith, creates a huge challenge for any Western country that might consider rescuing Uyghurs from Chinese oppression. Most other countries have also been victims of terrorism in one way or another. One way to address this problem would be to educate people on the type of Islamic faith that is embraced by Uyghurs. The majority of Uyghurs practice the moderate form of Sunni Islam blended with the local faith system, which is influenced by centuries of Sufism. A very small minority of Uyghurs ended up in Syria, after being deliberately allowed access to outside negative influence in China prior to embarking on their journey. This difference is critical because it provides a constructive way to counter the argument with China and provides substance to a condemnation of its indiscriminate suppression of Uyghurs in the name of anti-terrorism. This suppression includes children who have not yet formed any kind of religious awareness, knowledge, or worldview. China is deliberately blurring lines between Islamic faith and terrorists and, more specifically, between the majority moderate Uyghur Muslims and terrorists. It applies this sweeping accusation to all Uyghurs to justify its heavy-handed crackdown to the rest of China and the world.

The evidence that the CCP has presented to the world, painting Uyghurs with the brush of terrorism, is neither credible nor sustainable. For instance, the CCP uses the East Turkistan Islamic Movement (ETIM), now called the Turkistan Islamic Party (TIP), as an example of a key strategic threat to its national security. However, it is a shadowy organization that appears only when the CCP starts a new heavy-handed crackdown campaign and needs evidence of an imaginary threat. Critics say threats the TIP makes are exaggerated and that it is used by China to create a justification for an increase in the level of its crackdown on Uyghurs. This is all part of the psychological warfare that is used to deceive the world community. Dru C. Gladney, an authority on Uyghurs, said that there was a "credibility gap" about the group since the majority of information on it "was traced back to Chinese sources."[15]

TIP released a propaganda video in February of 2017 that appears to be the first to specifically threaten China, not in the Chinese language, but in Arabic. The film highlighted a division of Islamic State fighters with their family members in western Iraq, urging other TIP members to defect to Islamic State. Another fighter says explicitly that the Islamic State is coming to China, and the video features shots that appear to have been filmed in China.

In a recent *Washington Post* article, Sean Roberts, author of a forthcoming book on Uyghur militancy and an Associate Professor of the Practice of International Affairs at George Washington University, stated the video didn't appear to be aimed at recruiting Uyghurs, as it was mostly in Arabic with only limited Uyghur subtitles. He explains, "that made me wonder if it was more intended to send a message to China . . . It is unlikely that Uyghur extremists pose much of a concern to the United States, but there is also little evidence that ETIM was a viable organization when Beijing began to complain about it. It was only after years of harsh counterterrorism activity in Xinjiang that a diaspora of alienated Uyghurs emerged."[16]

At that time, China's Foreign Ministry said that it hoped the new video would prompt international cooperation for fighting Uyghur militants. A spokesman was quoted in the article, saying, "We have long said that East Turkestan forces are a serious threat to China's security, and we are willing to work with the international community to jointly crack down on East Turkestan separatist and terrorist forces."[17]

Shortly after that, in May of 2018, the world learned the secret of the camps in a bomb-shell revelation. Under the pressure of growing media and international interest, the CCP have repeatedly emphasized the threat of this shadowy organization. The TIP has long been used by China to paint all Uyghur grievances with the brush of terrorism, as they attempt to blame the whole Uyghur nation indiscriminately for their own treatment at the hands of the CCP.

One of the factors underlying the world's inability to stop the Uyghur genocide is that globalization is based around the principle of diplomacy. In working with countries to diplomatically resolve issues, there is one key ingredient missing from this equation when dealing with the CCP. When using diplomacy to raise concerns with a totalitarian state, any negotiations in good faith are one-sided. Because they recognize the sovereignty of China to manage its internal affairs, which is the current practice that the world is dealing economically with China and placing pressure on it mostly through economic means. For example, there are efforts to link issues of concern to certain trade conditions within the negotiation of the trade war with the US.

The problem with such an approach is that China is a world superpower economically, despite the CCP's totalitarian authority; therefore, no amount of economic pressure from other countries around the world is going to bring an end to the Uyghur genocide. The approach will be ineffective for two reasons: Firstly, no country in the world can create a significant enough downturn in China's economy through sanctions, and so on, without damaging their own country's economy. Even if it were possible, there would be huge pushback internally from all sectors of domestic business. Secondly, the CCP is happy to negotiate these terms in trade deals with the world, knowing that the world has no power to enforce them. Should the CCP choose not to abide by these terms, there is little other countries could do, given the diplomatic respect that they maintain for the sovereignty of China. The world, in the end, has no leverage—economic or otherwise—to hold China accountable for its crimes against humanity. The basic principles of diplomacy are founded in good faith, mutual benefits, and, above all, a balance of power. If these principles are not adhered to by all parties, then the country that breaks the faith gains everything and the country acting in good faith loses. The CCP is well aware of this, using it quite successfully so far with minimal resistance from the rest of the world.

To date, the response of the world has largely been to ignore it or turn a blind eye, mostly due to economics. It has painfully revealed that, in a globalized world, economic interests always have priority over human rights. The enlightenment ideals advocating liberty, progress, tolerance, fraternity, and constitutional government are shattered in the Uyghur genocide, just as they were shattered in the Holocaust, in Rwanda, and in Burma. Despite a growing number of testimonies from Uyghurs and Kazaks, the world has thus far failed to come to the aid of the victims of this genocide in the strictest sense of the word.

NOTES

1. "37 Countries Defend China Over Xinjiang In UN Letter," France24, Geneva AFP, July 12, 2019, https://www.france24.com/en/20190712-37-countries-defend-china-over-xinjiang-un-letter.

2. Aljazeera, "Saudi Crown Prince Defends China's Right to Fight 'Terrorism,'" Aljazeera, February 23, 2019, https://www.aljazeera.com/news/2019/02/saudi-crown-prince-defends-china-fight-terrorism-190223104647149.html.

3. Jamil Anderlini, "Chinese Muscle Stifles Criticism of Treatment of the Uighurs," *Financial Times*, May 1, 2019, https://www.ft.com/content/ebee2658-6b3c-11e9-80c7-60ee53e6681d.

4. Alim Seytoff and Joshua Lipes, "US Calls on UN to Demand Unfettered Access to Xinjiang to Investigate Reports of Rights Abuses," Radio Free Asia, September 24, 2019, https://www.rfa.org/english/news/uyghur/access-09242019171454.html/.

5. David Usborne, "UN Pilloried for Failure Over Rwanda Genocide," Independent, December 19, 1999, https://www.independent.co.uk/news/world/africa/un-pilloried-for-failure-over-rwanda-genocide-739072.html.

6. Aung San Suu Kyi, "Corrupted by Fear," *Washington Post*, October 15, 1991, https://www.washingtonpost.com/archive/opinions/1991/10/15/corrupted-by-fear/95604715-eb96-4f82-8808-9afd71eb0d88/.

7. "Statement by Concerned Scholars on China's Mass Detention of Turkic Minorities," November 26, 2018, https://concernedscholars.home.blog/.

8. James Griffiths, "US Lawmakers Say Trump Has Taken 'No Meaningful Action' Over China's Treatment of Muslims," CNN, March 5, 2019, https://edition.cnn.com/2019/03/04/politics/china-us-xinjiang-muslims-intl/index.html.

9. Uyghur Human Rights Policy Act of 2020, May 27, 2020, https://www.congress.gov/bill/116th-congress/senate-bill/3744.

10. Servet Günerigök, "US House Passes China Sanctions Bill on Uyghurs," Anadolu Agency, May 28, 2020, https://www.aa.com.tr/en/americas/us-house-passes-china-sanctions-bill-on-uyghurs/1855701.

11. Harry Cockburn, "Erik Prince: Blackwater Founder's New Company to Build 'Training Centre' in Chinese State Where Muslims Suffer Persecution," Independent, February 1, 2019, https://www.independent.co.uk/news/world/asia/erik-prince-china-reeducation-centres-xinjiang-uighur-muslims-blackwater-frontier-services-group-a8757871.html.

12. Johann Knox, "Proof of China's Organ Harvesting Found in Xinjiang: The Shocking Meaning Behind Kashgar Airport's 'Organ' Priority Lane," The Liberty Web, September 21, 2018, http://eng.the-liberty.com/2018/7286/.

13. Vicky Xiuzhong Xu, Danielle Cave, Dr James Leibold, Kelsey Munro, Nathan Ruser, "Uyghurs for Sale," The Australian Strategic Policy Institute Limited, March 1, 2020, https://www.aspi.org.au/report/uyghurs-sale.

14. Lianchao Han (Author), David Wong, Amelia Dewell and Anna Chen, "Cotton: The Fabric Full of Lies," Uyghur Human Rights Project, August 27, 2019, https://uhrp.org/news-commentary/report-released-cotton-fabric-full-lies.

15. Ritt Goldstein, "Freed from Guantánamo, a Uighur Clings to Asylum Dreams in Sweden," The Christian Science Monitor, April 24, 2009, https://www.csmonitor.com/World/2009/0424/p06s04-wogn.html.

16. Adam Taylor, "How Trump Could Find Common Ground with China, Thanks to the Islamic State," *Washington Post*, March 2, 2017, https://www.washingtonpost.com/news/worldviews/wp/2017/03/02/how-donald-trump-could-find-common-ground-with-china-thanks-to-the-islamic-state/.

17. Ibid.

Chapter Nine

Beyond Death and Destruction

What win I, if I gain the thing I seek?
A dream, a breath, a froth of fleeting joy.
Who buys a minute's mirth to wail a week?
Or sells eternity to get a toy?
For one sweet grape who will the vine destroy?
Or what fond beggar, but to touch the crown,
Would with the sceptre straight be strucken down?

—William Shakespeare

Gene A. Bunin conducted a series of interviews with Uyghurs in China, using the material in an article that was published in *The Guardian* in 2018, entitled "We Are a People Destroyed: Why Uighur Muslims across China Are Living in Fear." The article describes a pervasive sense of desperation among Uyghurs in Kashgar, the heart of Uyghur culture, as follows:

On a few occasions, I encountered people who seemed to have reached a degree of desperation, and just wanted to let everything out. The first such time was in Kashgar, in autumn last year, when a uniformed public-security worker—the mostly Uighur, lowest-rank uniformed authority in southern Xinjiang—invited me to sit across from him at a table in a teahouse. He was off duty that afternoon, having just returned from a medical checkup.

The conversation that followed was tense. He asked me what I knew of Uighur history, and then asked me what I thought of the Uighurs as a people. The latter question is one I have been asked several times during my years in Xinjiang and has often struck me as a way of searching for some sort of outside verification of Uighurs' identity. Unsure of how to reply, I tried to be noncommittal: "The Uighurs are a people like any other, with their good and bad."

"You're hiding what you really think," he confronted me. "Just look all around you. You've seen it yourself [here in Kashgar]. We're a people destroyed."[1]

The situation in Kashgar has deteriorated drastically since then. What strikes me in this conversation is the doubt of the interlocutor, uncertain and unable to vocalize the identity of Uyghurs as a people destroyed. I know that it is as painful to hear this as it is to say it. Yet, the reality is, the people are destroyed, and they know they are a people being destroyed. The self-consciousness of this destruction is tragic in two senses—knowing it in the form of collective self-consciousness while being powerless to change it. This knowledge spins perpetually and continually in the minds and hearts of Uyghurs daily, while their destruction continues endlessly and silently outside of themselves, outside of their realm of control. This is the saddest form of self-knowledge that the collective self is being destroyed while experiencing it painfully in detail.

If these people are destroyed, what could any future possibly be for them? How could the destroyed rise from the ashes? How could they continue to exist, getting themselves together, overcoming the collective intergenerational trauma, reviving their vitality to rejuvenate themselves and come to terms with their tormentors one day, if such a thing is even possible?

More importantly, the destroyer of Uyghurs is not yet destroyed. It is still aggressive, continuing to commit genocide and slyly deceiving the world about its grossly immoral actions. There is no end in sight to see Uyghurs freed from the concentration camps and slave labor factories at this stage. While being freed would be an improvement over their current circumstances, they would then enter back into Chinese society, which is also equipped with advanced technologies to cage, monitor, silence, and control them. China has accumulated considerable experience in terrorizing Uyghurs. What or who would stop them from putting Uyghurs back in concentration camps in the name of re-education or in prisons or in factories using Uyghur slave laborers at any time, based on any imaginary crime or virus they choose?

Further, the accusations that the CCP has leveled against Uyghurs are still "valid" in their minds. They will continue to use them against Uyghur dissent and grievances, however minor, to justify the harsh crackdown. These accusations are like a noose around the neck of Uyghurs as the labels of terrorists and criminals.

With rare access to the camps granted by the Chinese government, the BBC journalist John Sudworth created a short documentary film entitled *Inside China's "Thought Transformation" Camps*. Zhang Zhisheng from Xinjiang Foreign Affairs Office stated: "Some people, before they commit murder, already show they are capable of killing. Should we wait for them to commit the crime? Or should we prevent it from happening?"[2] This comment reveals that in the eyes of Chinese officials, most Uyghurs already harbor murderous desires on a massive scale. Chinese authorities apparently "knew" their potential before it was actualized. If the CCP already has the capacity to see what goes on in the minds of Uyghurs, one wonders why they need the surveillance and the camps to infiltrate their thoughts. Why do they not rename the camps more properly as crime-prevention centers, rather than re-education centers? If the government is omnipotent to the point of knowing what people think, then why have they not prevented all crimes in China and turned it into the first crime-free country on Earth? Zhang's comment confirms that CCP officials consider Uyghurs indiscriminately as potential criminals because they are potential terrorists. In fact, both accusations stem from the same source of stigma: Uyghurs are terrorists and, hence, murderers.

These accusations are psychological as well as political traps for Uyghurs. Any Uyghur resistance against the CCP's oppression, now or in the future, will be seen through the lenses of terrorism and crime-mindedness. While their struggle for freedom from tyranny is being misconstrued as the actions of terrorists or murderers, they continue to risk imprisonment for the arbitrary and illegal charge of having alleged murderous intent. These charges will continue to hang over them until they are assimilated or annihilated. If they resist, they are murdered for being a potential murderer; if they cease resisting, they are still destined to perish. It is a catch-22: they will always be condemned and imprisoned, either because they have resisted and are therefore clearly terrorists, or because they have cooperated and are then sent to be re-educated. Either way, their political kismet is elimination.

Uyghurs now collectively live in fear of potential terrorism charges by the CCP. Given the world's silence, they have good reason to fear further brutality if they retaliate against the CCP. Indeed, they are aware that the CCP would welcome these actions as new evidence that Uyghurs are, as it has said for years, dangerous terrorists. They are also aware that no other country has ever supported their political goal of independence, which is a forbidden dream and further fuels the resentment of the CCP and Han Chinese against Uyghurs. If they abandon this dream, Uyghurs don't know what kind of a meaningful future is awaiting them. Even if this genocide ends with some of them left alive, they will have no other option than to continue living under the tyranny of the CCP. Then, the most inconvenient question arises—what will be the difference between dying in the process of genocide or being kept alive in such a murderous regime?

The critical question Uyghurs must ask themselves is this: if their religious faith is one of the main reasons they are subject to this genocide, what should they do? Should Uyghurs denounce their faith, reconcile their faith with the requirements of the CCP, or keep believing in their faith with the courage to face any consequences? This is a real dilemma for Uyghurs. For a people destroyed, religion is one of the last spiritual sanctuaries. Uyghurs, who have lost their land, culture, and all their rights, will naturally withdraw back into their faith as spiritual solace. In their extreme solitude, only religion keeps them sane and hopeful, something to cling on to in the vast and treacherous sea, in which they are collectively drowning. This religion, however much peace and solace it may bring them, is the source of the accusations and condemnation against them by the CCP, the reason they are labeled as terrorists. For the CCP, Islam is a religion of terror. Therefore, Islam is the eternal dilemma of Uyghurs as long as they live under the tyranny of the CCP. If they abandon it, which is extremely difficult to imagine, they lose the reason for their spiritual existence; if they continue to embrace it, they will never escape the CCP's accusations of terrorism.

From a global perspective, counterterrorism is one of the critical national security issues for almost all countries. While there are many differences among these countries in their perceptions and definitions of what constitutes terrorism and how to respond to it, there is a consensus that some Muslims and Islamic factions may harbor terrorist tendencies. This potential, with its fresh possibilities, continues to breed Islamophobia. When Islamophobia influences counterterrorism strategies, even in part, then it is difficult to ensure an approach that is proportionate and unbiased. Currently, the counterterrorism policies of some countries are deeply Islamophobic. These policies advocate for exclusion instead of inclusion, promote hatred instead of compassion, and increasing generalization instead of individualization. In the end, they quickly create a picture of evil, vilifying almost all Muslims as an object of hatred. In the current global political climate, many politicians can benefit from condemning Muslims to encourage support from right-wing extremists.

The Uyghur genocide must be viewed and understood within this international context. The CCP is well aware that it is not difficult to paint Uyghurs collectively as terrorists by hijacking the sentiments of Islamophobia, ensuring a lack of sympathy for the punishment Uyghurs endure on account of their Islamic faith. They have been encouraged by the international community's lack of response to other violence, war, and genocides in Yemen, Syria, and Burma. Seeing this, the CCP became confident the international community would have a similar response—or lack of response—when they became aware of their violence against Uyghurs. The timing of the genocide was well-calculated and deliberately chosen to occur in the middle of the Syrian conflicts and Rohingya genocide, and the lack of uproar confirmed the world's Islamophobic belief that it will be far safer with fewer Muslims.

The CCP's counterterrorism measures still have a long way to go to reach their ultimate goals, so China may not be able to continue using this tactic until all Uyghurs are subsumed into its will or eliminated. Even if the CCP cannot convince the world that Uyghurs are terrorists indefinitely, it has another card to play as it has never been short of these cards. The next card is a bit inconvenient but still useful—it involves labeling Uyghurs as separatists. In the end, whatever Uyghurs do, inside or outside of China, peaceful or not, they remain condemned to be terrorists, a label effectively concealing the state-sponsored terrorism of China against them. Whatever they do, Uyghurs will continually fall into a guilt trap constructed of terrorism charges leveled against them.

Opposite to the terrorist's trap, Uyghurs also find themselves in the firm grip of the savior's trap. Unlike the Nazis, who openly declared their plan to murder all Jews, the CCP has never declared its plan to eliminate all Uyghurs. Instead, it continues to defend its deadly plan in highly contradictory ways, with claims that it is saving Uyghurs from criminal ideas and cleansing them from a fatal terrorist virus. While this justification forms the "logical" basis of the whole *modus operandi* of the genocide, it is deeply paradoxical that the CCP is claiming to save Uyghurs by killing them. This justification creates the savior's trap that is difficult for Uyghurs to escape from. It can be applied to any Uyghur at any time, depending, as it does, on the unproven contents of their minds. This approach has allowed China to successfully establish an increasingly vast network of concentration camps without much resistance.

The prospect of all Uyghurs being released from the camps is very unlikely at best. Likely, only those Uyghurs who are utterly brainwashed or broken to the point where they are no longer a "threat" will be released. When brainwashing is not successful, they will most likely permanently disappear, be given long jail sentences, or be forced to do slave labor. Even if they are all released, it is unlikely they would have the capacity to lead independent and productive lives, given the post-traumatic stress they will no doubt be suffering. In addition, the surveillance cameras, aggressive and racist police, and the hate-filled eyes of Han Chinese will still be there. Anyone who has survived and been released from the camps and from the prisons will have surely lost their sense of reality and will struggle to distinguish between the camp and the outside world.

The prospect of Uyghurs' widespread, successful release is further diminished when one considers the repressive measures the CCP is frantically using to hide its crimes from the world. When any camp inmate is released, he or she must sign an agreement that states they will never tell anybody about what they experienced inside the camps. How long can the CCP ensure that information about its crimes in the camps is kept secret? The CCP has already murdered many Uyghurs inside the camps as testimonies have confirmed. Current evidence supports the grim likelihood that the CCP is continuing and even escalating their actions against Uyghurs as time passes. This escalation is not due to the CCP's fear of being caught red-handed but is merely a reflection of their determination. After all, the mission of eliminating every Uyghur is not yet complete. To the CCP, a half-accomplished mission is a disastrous mission, for it still leaves some room—however small—for information about its crime to leak out. Unless the source of this potential leakage—Uyghur victims—is destroyed, it is still possible that the CCP will be brought to justice one day. Behind walls of the concentration camps and prisons, the CCP will continue killing Uyghurs to suppress them and their voices permanently. Then, it will turn to other Uyghurs overseas until there is no Uyghur left in the world as a last witness for its crimes against humanity.

Is there any hope for Uyghurs in this time of prolonged destruction and profound loss that reaches across generations? They lost their motherland long ago, reluctantly accepting they were collectively captive in their ancestral home. They have now lost their religious rights, heritage, tradition, institutions, and figures, and are forcibly transformed into atheists with Chinese characteristics. They have lost their language, a means of cultural expression that has been used by their ancestors for centuries, as they are forbidden to speak Uyghur. They have lost their next generation, the children who are separated from their parents and deeply traumatized, without knowing what the future holds for them. They have lost their sense of security, living in surveillance state, scrutinized by omnipresent security cameras, tracked down anywhere and anytime. They have lost their minds in the concentration camps and prisons through thought transformation, which has turned them into slaves and, eventually, zombies. They have lost their health while sedated and helpless, as their organs are removed and sold on the market as precious commodities. They have lost their faith in the world, which abandoned them when they needed help most desperately.

Our life in exile is barely better than that of Uyghurs at home, either inside or outside the camps. We are dying on the inside, perhaps not physically but spiritually. Destruction in the camps is radiating outward to us, and we feel as if we are trapped in an emotional camp. We are still running away, in our nightmares, from the horror occurring in our homeland. There was an article published recently in *The Australian,* called "Mother pleads for help to end 'Uyghur nightmare.'" Ms. Zulfia Erk described the experience this way: "I feel helpless and hopeless. We are seeking a peaceful life but our life is not in peace, mentally we are not in peace. All night I have to fight with my nightmares and then I know the world doesn't care."[3]

One of my friends asked me the other day if I had considered the prospect of eventually forgiving Chinese people involved in the Uyghur genocide. I replied, "Why should the weak, the accused, and the destroyed consider forgiveness in the first place?" "Yeah," said he, "forgiveness is a great virtue, and it requires your courage, as you know." I was surprised and went on to say, "Yes, it is. It means there is something in me, more than just the courage. It means that I have something invincible in me that will make the killers seek forgiveness for their crimes. As long as I exist, I will never forget the massive destruction they have brought to my people. One day, Uyghurs may forgive their perpetrators, not for their benefit, but showing that their spirit is far bigger and stronger than destruction. They will show Han Chinese how the monstrosity in the depth of their minds has corrupted their ability to accept their responsibility for terrible destruction to their own souls as well that will haunt them forever across their generations. In the end, they will admit that, in destroying Uyghurs, they have destroyed all the precious ideas and humane feelings in their own souls."

Forgiveness may be seen as selfish. It is something you do to live more comfortably with yourself, if not to live with the perpetrator. It is something you do to heal your own pain and suffering. Moreover, it is a preventative measure ensuring your moral values are not reducing you to the same level as your abusers. It is a confirmation of your ethical and moral code. It is not a celebration of the triumph of good over evil; instead, it is a choice made independently of the battle. Forgiveness can mean the acceptance of weakness, not only of the victims but also of goodness. It is a sign of extreme vulnerability, wherein the victims demonstrate to the perpetrators they are alive, and their soul remains invincible, even while many other lives and souls have been senselessly taken. The act of forgiveness is deeply contradictory as it is a sign of both the resilience and fragility of human life. On this note, I will also never forget what Viktor E. Frankl, a Holocaust survivor, said:

> We who lived in concentration camps can remember the men who walked through the huts comforting others, giving away their last piece of bread. They may have been few in number, but they offer sufficient proof that everything can be taken away from a man but one thing. The last of the human freedoms—to choose one's attitude in any given circumstances, and to choose one's own way.[4]

The essence of Uyghur suffering lies in their unquenchable longing for freedom. If not for that, they might have already given up under the weight of endless oppression and accepted being Han Chinese. Succumbing would not only have prevented their death and destruction, but it would also have allowed them the status of full-fledged participants in the cultural and political life of an economically strong yet politically repressive country. Nevertheless, Uyghurs have constantly refused assimilation into this country, this culture, and its ruling party, the CCP. They preferred being Uyghur to being Han Chinese, even though this preference meant almost certain destruction. Even in the midst of this ongoing disaster, many Uyghurs in exile remain determined to overcome the CCP's tyranny one day and, finally, experience the freedom of being Uyghurs in their motherland.

People may wonder if it is reasonable or wise to seek such seemingly distant freedom when the struggle is bringing such existential calamity to

Uyghurs now. To me, it is this freedom-seeking spirit of Uyghurs keeping them moving forward by maintaining their unique culture, faith, and material wealth. This same spirit has made Uyghurs an archenemy of the state of China. Just as there would be no point in life for Uyghurs without freedom seeking, China's nationalistic drive for world domination via a fully Sinicized state has equal primacy for them. Prioritizing their agenda, the CCP is obsessed with destroying the freedom-seeking spirit in Uyghurs from cradle to grave. Is freedom too costly for Uyghurs? Only time will provide the answer. The freedom-seeking spirit will either sustain their determination or lead to their further annihilation. Even if Uyghurs are totally eliminated, it will remain their choice to not become Han Chinese in the end.

Here is the ultimate question: can Uyghurs and Han Chinese live together during and after this destruction? At this stage, it is hard to imagine this type of socio-cultural, if not political, harmony, at least for Uyghurs in exile. There is one crucial point to consider. The two cultures cannot begin to live together until they decide their political future by uniting against the source of evil, the CCP. This political organization, having no legal legitimacy, is suppressing everybody in China. It is killing Uyghurs, but it is also denying the human rights of Han Chinese and others. As long as the CCP still exists, it will continue to suppress Uyghurs and use Han Chinese for its own purposes as post-modern slaves with its sophisticated surveillance technologies and repressive measures. Eventually, China will become a full-fledged dystopian country, where no one can challenge its pervasive, deep-rooted, and omnipotent authority.

Currently, the CCP is pitting Uyghurs against Han Chinese by fanning the nationalistic feelings of the latter. This strategy of divide-and-rule prevents any unified assault against the CCP. If the hatred between Uyghurs and Han Chinese persists, then the CCP will effortlessly ride this momentum, suppressing any internal resistance and gradually extending its menacing power of suppression into other regions and countries.

It is the responsibility of the international community as a whole to help Uyghurs and Han Chinese come together to form a unified front and resist against the CCP. If not, the CCP—which is eliminating Uyghurs and suppressing Han Chinese today—will eventually bring the fight to the rest of the world. The spread of COVID-19, which plunged the whole world into deep pain and suffering, should be a wake-up call. It allows the world to see what the CCP, with its tendency to cover up and manipulate the truth, means for humanity. The COVID-19 pandemic could have been far less severe all around the world, if the CCP had been transparent. The leaders of the CCP instead chose to suppress the reports of doctors and researchers who sought to raise the alarm. Evidence of the outbreak was destroyed, the facts were denied, and the world was left with no reliable clues as to how dangerous this virus was and could be.

In the midst of this global pandemic, we must notice the similarity between the behaviors of the CCP in the Uyghur crisis and their handling of the pandemic. Just as it lied about the concentration camps at the beginning of 2018, so it is still lying about how and where this virus spread in the first place and what the real number of symptomatic and asymptomatic cases is, etc. Just as it described the Uyghur genocide as a benign campaign by a would-be savior, so it now proudly reports the provision of faulty medical equipment for virus-ridden countries such as Italy, Spain, and Turkey as an act of support and assistance. The same old savior syndrome with Chinese characteristics is showing its monstrous face to the world. Now, it is time to expose the real danger of the CCP, which still has an enormous capacity to do additional damage to humankind.

The world does not currently recognize the level of cruelty and destruction inflicted by the genocide in the Uyghur homeland. Therefore, they also fail to recognize the larger implications of this situation, specifically the imminent threat the CCP poses to the rest of the world. For many people, Uyghurs in concentration camps sound like a myth, too surreal or too bizarre to believe. Some have even said it must be a lie or exaggeration used to vilify China. Now, if we look at how the world has been turned upside down due to the spread of COVID-19, which has brought global lockdowns, forced millions of people to stay home, and caused many to lose their lives, jobs, families and communities, the vision of concentration camps is no longer so far from reality. The CCP has committed similar crimes against Uyghurs, and will continue to commit more crimes against others, so long as no one has the moral courage to oppose them or support those who do, and so take vital action to stop it. The world must realize that the inherent violence of the CCP will certainly not end exclusively with the destruction of Uyghurs.

NOTES

1. Gene A Bunin "'We're a People Destroyed': Why Uighur Muslims Across China Are Living in Fear," *The Guardian*, August 7, 2018, https://www.theguardian.com/news/2018/aug/07/why-uighur-muslims-across-china-are-living-in-fear.

2. BBC News, *Inside China's "Thought Transformation" Camps*, YouTube video, 11:58, June 18, 2019, https://www.youtube.com/watch?v=WmId2ZP3h0c.

3. Primrose Riordan, "Mother Pleads for Help to End Uighurs' 'Nightmare,'" *The Australian*, August 21, 2018, https://www.theaustralian.com.au/national-affairs/mother-pleads-for-help-to-end-uighurs-nightmare/news-story/caaf85b8b5b8d312aa83424cf7f808e4.

4. Viktor E. Frankl, *Man's Search for Meaning* (New York: Pocket Books, 1985), 86.

Bibliography

Ala, Mamtimin, "Turn in the Two-Faced: The Plight of Uyghur Intellectuals," *The Diplomat*, October 12, 2018, https://thediplomat.com/2018/10/turn-in-the-two-faced-the-plight-of-uyghur-intellectuals/.

Aljazeera, "Saudi Crown Prince Defends China's Right to Fight 'Terrorism,'" Aljazeera, February 23, 2019, https://www.aljazeera.com/news/2019/02/saudi-crown-prince-defends-china-fight-terrorism-190223104647149.html.

Anderlini, Jamil, "Chinese Muscle Stifles Criticism of Treatment of the Uighurs," *Financial Times*, May 1, 2019, https://www.ft.com/content/ebee2658-6b3c-11e9-80c7-60ee53e6681d.

AsiaNews, "The Uyghur Men Jailed in Mass Arrests in Xinjiang," June 19, 2018, http://www.asianews.it/news-en/Uyghur-men-jailed-in-mass-arrests-in-Xinjiang-44210.html.

BBC News, "China Uighurs: Xinjiang Ban on Long Beards and Veils," BBC, April 1, 2017, https://www.bbc.com/news/world-asia-china-39460538.

BBC News, *Inside China's "Thought Transformation" Camps*, YouTube video, 11:58, June 18, 2019, https://www.youtube.com/watch?v=WmId2ZP3h0c.

Buckley, Chris, "China Is Detaining Muslims in Vast Numbers. The Goal: 'Transformation,'" *New York Times*, September 8, 2018, https://www.nytimes.com/2018/09/08/world/asia/china-uighur-muslim-detention-camp.html.

Bunin, Gene A., "'We're a People Destroyed': Why Uighur Muslims across China Are Living in Fear," *The Guardian*, August 7, 2018, https://www.theguardian.com/news/2018/aug/07/why-uighur-muslims-across-china-are-living-in-fear.

Byler, Darren, "'The Night Is Thick': Uyghur Poets Respond to the Disappearance of Their Relatives," SupChina, March 6, 2019, https://supchina.com/2019/03/06/uyghur-poets-respond-to-the-disappearance-of-their-relatives/.

Chao, Steve, "Exposed: China's Surveillance of Muslim Uighurs," Turkistantimes, Aljazeera, Feb 1, 2019, http://turkistantimes.com/en/news-10066.html.

China Change, "A Call for a UN Investigation, and US Sanctions, on the Human Rights Disaster Unfolding in Xinjiang," August 10, 2018, https://chinachange.org/2018/08/10/a-call-for-a-un-investigation-and-us-sanctions-on-the-human-rights-disaster-unfolding-in-xinjiang/.

Cockburn, Harry, "Erik Prince: Blackwater Founder's New Company to Build 'Training Centre' in Chinese State Where Muslims Suffer Persecution," Independent, February 1, 2019, https://www.independent.co.uk/news/world/asia/erik-prince-china-reeducation-centres-xinjiang-uighur-muslims-blackwater-frontier-services-group-a8757871.html.

Concerned Scholars Home, "Statement by Concerned Scholars on China's Mass Detention of Turkic Minorities," November 26, 2018, https://concernedscholars.home.blog/

Confucius, "The Analects," in *A Source Book in Chinese Philosophy*, ed. Wing-Tsit Chan, Princeton, NJ: Princeton University Press, 1973.

Congressional-Executive Commission on China, "Regional Ethnic Autonomy Law of the People's Republic of China," amended February 28, 2001, https://www.cecc.gov/resources/legal-provisions/regional-ethnic-autonomy-law-of-the-peoples-republic-of-china-amended.

Doman, Mark, Stephen Hutcheon, Dylan Welch, and Kyle Taylor, "China's Frontier of Fear," ABC News, November 1, 2018, https://www.abc.net.au/news/2018-11-01/satellite-images-expose-chinas-network-of-re-education-camps/10432924.

Fine, Gail, *The Oxford Handbook of Plato*, Second Edition, Oxford, Oxford University Press, 2019.

France24, Geneva AFP, "37 Countries Defend China Over Xinjiang in UN Letter," July 12, 2019, https://www.france24.com/en/20190712-37-countries-defend-china-over-xinjiang-un-letter.

Frankl, Viktor E., *Man's Search for Meaning*, New York: Pocket Books, 1985.

Goldstein, Ritt, "Freed from Guantánamo, a Uighur Clings to Asylum Dreams in Sweden," The Christian Science Monitor, April 24, 2009, https://www.csmonitor.com/World/2009/0424/p06s04-wogn.html.

Graham-Harrison, Emma and Juliette Garside, "'Allow No Escapes': Leak Exposes Reality of China's Vast Prison Camp Network," *The Guardian*, Guardian News and Media, November 24, 2019, https://www.theguardian.com/world/2019/nov/24/china-cables-leak-no-escapes-reality-china-uighur-prison-camp.

Griffiths, James, "US Lawmakers Say Trump Has Taken 'No Meaningful Action' Over China's Treatment of Muslims," CNN, March 5, 2019, https://edition.cnn.com/2019/03/04/politics/china-us-xinjiang-muslims-intl/index.html.

Günerigök, Servet, "US House Passes China Sanctions Bill on Uyghurs," Anadolu Agency, May 28, 2020, https://www.aa.com.tr/en/americas/us-house-passes-china-sanctions-bill-on-uyghurs/1855701.

Han, Lianchao (Author), David Wong, Amelia Dewell and Anna Chen, "Cotton: The Fabric Full of Lies," Uyghur Human Rights Project, August 27, 2019, https://uhrp.org/news-commentary/report-released-cotton-fabric-full-lies.

Huang, Yunte (ed.), *The Big Red Book of Modern Chinese Literature: Writings from the Mainland in the Long Twentieth Century*, New York: W.W. Norton & Company, 2016.

Human Rights Watch, "'Eradicating Ideological Viruses': China's Campaign of Repression Against Xinjiang's Muslims," September 9, 2018, https://www.hrw.org/report/2018/09/09/eradicating-ideological-viruses/chinas-campaign-repression-against-xinjiangs.

Human Rights Watch, "China: Visiting Officials Occupy Homes in Muslim Region," May 13, 2018, https://www.hrw.org/news/2018/05/13/china-visiting-officials-occupy-homes-muslim-region.

International Uyghur Human Rights & Democracy Foundation, "China's 21st Century Internment Camps in the Uyghur Region," August 20, 2018, http://www.iuhrdf.org/content/china's-21st-century-internment-camps-uyghur-region.

Knox, Johann, "Proof of China's Organ Harvesting Found in Xinjiang: The Shocking Meaning Behind Kashgar Airport's 'Organ' Priority Lane," The Liberty Web, September 21, 2018, http://eng.the-liberty.com/2018/7286/.

Kozaric'-Kovac˘ic', Dragica, Vera Folnegovic'-S˘malc, and Jarmila S˘krinjaric', "Systematic Raping of Women in Croatia and Bosnia and Herzegovina: A Preliminary Psychiatric Report," *Croatian Medical Journal* 34 (1995): 87–88.

Kozaric'-Kovac˘ic', Dragica, Vera Folnegovic'-S˘malc, Jarmila S˘krinjaric', Nathan M. Szajnberg, and Ana Marusic', "Rape, Torture and Traumatization of Bosnian and Croatian Women: Psychological Sequelae," *American Journal of Orthopsychiatry* 65 (1995): 428–33.

Kuo, Lily, "From Denial to Pride: How China Changed Its Language on Xinjiang's Camps," *The Guardian*, October 22, 2018, https://www.theguardian.com/world/2018/oct/22/from-denial-to-pride-how-china-changed-its-language-on-xinjiangs-camps.

Kymlicka, Will and Baogang He, *Multiculturalism in Asia*, Oxford: Oxford University Press, 2005, https://doi.org/10.1093/0199277621.001.0001.

Le Bon, Gustave, *The Crowd: A Study of the Popular Mind*, Auckland: The Floating Press, 2009.

Leithead, Alastair, "Stanford Prison Experiment Continues to Shock," BBC News, August 17, 2011, https://www.bbc.com/news/world-us-canada-14564182.

Levinas, Emmanuel, *Nine Talmudic Readings*, Bloomington: Indiana University Press, 1994.

Lim, Louisa, "China: Reengineering the Uighur," The Interpreter, Lowy Institute, November 7, 2018, https://www.lowyinstitute.org/the-interpreter/China-re-engineer-uighur.

Lixiong, Wang, "Excerpts from 'My West China and Your East Turkestan'—My View on the Kunming Incident," March 3, 2014, https://chinachange.org/2014/03/03/excerpts-from-my-west-china-your-east-Turkistan-my-view-on-the-kunming-incident/.

Mencius, "The Book of Mencius," in Chan, *A Source Book*, 52.

Mostafa, Mohamed and Mohamed Nagi, "'They Are Not Welcome': Report on the Uyghur Crisis in Egypt," Association of Freedom of Thought and Expression October, Egyptian Commission for Rights and Freedoms, October 1, 2017, https://afteegypt.org/en/academ ic_freedoms/2017/10/01/13468-afteegypt.html.

Nebehay, Stephanie, "U.N. Says It Has Credible Reports that China Holds Million Uighurs in Secret Camps," Reuters, August 12, 2018, https://www.reuters.com/article/us-china-rights-un/u-n-says-it-has-credible-reports-that-china-holds-million-uighurs-in-secret-camps-idUSKBN1KV1SU.

Nietzsche, Friedrich, *Human, All Too Human: A Book for a Free Spirit,* Part II, New York: The MacMillan Company, 1913.

Nosthoff, Anna-Verena, "Barbarism: Notes on the Thought of Theodor W. Adorno," Critical Legal Thinking, 15 October 2014, https://criticallegalthinking.com/2014/10/15/barbarism-notes-thought-theodor-w-adorno/.

Orwell, George, *Animal Farm and 1984*, Boston: Harcourt Books, 2003.

Osnos, Evan, *Age of Ambition: Chasing Fortune, Truth and Faith in the New China*, New York: Farrar, Straus and Giroux, 2015.

Radio Free Asia, "Xinjiang Authorities Push Uyghurs to Marry Han Chinese," 2017, https://www.rfa.org/english/news/special/uyghur-oppression/ChenPolicy2.html.

Radio Free Europe/Radio Liberty, "Uyghur Man Stabbed to Death in South China," January 9, 2010, https://www.rferl.org/a/Uyghur_Man_Stabbed_To_Death_In_South_China/ 1924768.html.

Ramzy, Austin and Chris Buckley. "'Absolutely No Mercy': Leaked Files Expose How China Organized Mass Detentions of Muslims," *New York Times*, November 16, 2019, https://www.nytimes.com/interactive/2019/11/16/world/asia/china-xinjiang-documents.html.

Riordan, Primrose, "Mother Pleads for Help to End Uighurs' 'Nightmare,'" *The Australian*, August 21, 2018, https://www.theaustralian.com.au/national-affairs/mother-pleads-for-help-to-end-uighurs-nightmare/news-story/caaf85b8b5b8d312aa83424cf7f808e4.

Rosen, Alan (ed.), *Literature of the Holocaust*, New York: Cambridge University Press, 2013.

Rosenthal, Alan, "Eichmann, Revisited," *The Jerusalem Post*, April 20, 2011, https://www.jpost.com/Jerusalem-Report/Jewish-World/Eichmann-Revisited.

Şafak, Yeni, "Chinese Internment Camps Are 'Torture Centers Worse than Death,' Say Survivors," last modified December 8, 2018, https://www.yenisafak.com/en/world/chinese-internment-camps-are-torture-centers-that-are-worse-than-death-say-survivors-3468651.

Sales, Nathan and Sam Brownback, "Opinion: China's Attack on Uighurs Isn't Counterterrorism. It's Ugly Repression," *Washington Post*, WP Company, May 22, 2019, https://www.washingtonpost.com/opinions/chinas-attack-on-uighurs-isnt-counterterrorism-its-ugly-repression/2019/05/22/7bfb1d60-7ccb-11e9-a5b3-34f3edf1351e_story.html.

Seytoff, Alim and Joshua Lipes, "Expert Estimates China Has More Than 1000 Internment Camps for Xinjiang Uyghurs," Radio Free Asia, November 13, 2019.

Seytoff, Alim and Joshua Lipes, "US Calls on UN to Demand Unfettered Access to Xinjiang to Investigate Reports of Rights Abuses," Radio Free Asia, September 24, 2019, https://www.rfa.org/english/news/uyghur/access-09242019171454.html/.

Shih, Gerry, "China's Mass Indoctrination Camps Evoke Cultural Revolution," AP News, *Associated Press*, May 18, 2018, https://www.apnews.com/ 6e151296fb194f85ba69a8babd972e4b.

Sidiq, Erkin, "Latest Information about Uyghurs in East Turkestan," Uighur Times, July 6, 2019, https://uighurtimes.com/index.php/latest-information-about-uyghurs-in-east-turkestan/.

Stewart, Phil, "China Putting Minority Muslims in 'Concentration Camps,' U.S. Says," Reuters, May 3, 2019, https://www.reuters.com/article/us-usa-china-concentrationcamps/china-putting-minority-muslims-in-concentration-camps-us-says-idUSKCN1S925K.

Suu Kyi, Aung San, "Corrupted by Fear," *Washington Post*, October 15, 1991, https://www.washingtonpost.com/archive/opinions/1991/10/15/corrupted-by-fear/95604715-eb96-4f82-8808-9afd71eb0d88/.

Szadziewski, Henryk, "Disappeared Forever?" China Channel, February 28, 2019, https://chinachannel.org/2019/02/21/uighur-eliticide/.

Taylor, Adam, "How Could Trump Find Common Ground with China, Thanks to the Islamic State," *Washington Post*, March 2, 2017, https://www.washingtonpost.com/news/worldviews/wp/2017/03/02/how-donald-trump-could-find-common-ground-with-china-thanks-to-the-islamic-state/.

Thum, Rian, "How an American TV Show Captured the Extent of Chinese Repression," *Washington Post*, May 9, 2019, https://www.washingtonpost.com/opinions/2019/05/09/how-an-american-tv-show-captured-extent-chinese-repression/.

Tze, Hsün, "The Book of Hsün Tze," in Chan, *A Source Book*, 28.

Usborne, David, "UN Pilloried for Failure Over Rwanda Genocide," Independent, December 19, 1999, https://www.independent.co.uk/news/world/africa/un-pilloried-for-failure-over-rwanda-genocide-739072.html.

Uyghur Human Rights Policy Act of 2020, May 27, 2020, https://www.congress.gov/bill/116th-congress/senate-bill/3744.

Van Brugen, Isabel, "Former Uyghur Inmates Tell of Torture and Rape in China's 'Re-Education' Camps," *The Epoch Times*, October 15, 2018, https://www.theepochtimes.com/former-uyghur-inmates-tell-of-torture-and-rape-in-chinas-re-education-camps_2689053.html.

Walker, Heidi Anne, "How and Why I Write: Interview with Wiesel," *Journal of Education* 2, 119, Boston University, 1980.

Werleman, CJ, "How Uyghurs Are Silenced from Sharing Their Suffering with the World," TRT World, May 14, 2019, https://www.trtworld.com/opinion/how-uyghurs-are-silenced-from-sharing-their-suffering-with-the-world-26636.

Werleman, CJ, "New Horrors: China Harvesting Muslim Organs in Concentration Camps," Extra Newsfeed, April 6, 2019, https://extranewsfeed.com/new-horrors-china-harvesting-muslim-organs-in-concentration-camps-9a252d3c373e?gi=f0b0ef3019e.

Wiesel, Elie, Lucy S. Dawidowitz, Dorothy Rabinowitz and Robert McAfee Brown (1990), "Dimensions of the Holocaust," Northwestern University Press, 7.

Xu, Vicky Xiuzhong, Danielle Cave, Dr. James Leibold, Kelsey Munro and Nathan Ruser, "Uyghurs for Sale," The Australian Strategic Policy Institute Limited, March 1, 2020, https://www.aspi.org.au/report/uyghurs-sale.

Yutang, Lin, *My Country and My People*, London: William Heineman LTD, 1936.

Index

About the Author

Born on November 7, 1971, in Atush, East Turkistan (aka the Xinjiang Uyghur Autonomous Region of China), Mamtimin Ala is, at heart, a humanitarian who has a PhD in philosophy successfully achieved at Katholieke Universiteit Leuven in Belgium in June 2010 with *magna cum laude*, and his thesis focus was on the notion of identity and anonymity. Professionally, he has worked in many diverse roles internationally, including as a research analyst at Human Rights Without Frontiers in 2006 in Belgium in the field of international human rights.

In 2008, Mamtimin migrated to Australia after he was granted political asylum where he worked as manager for a settlement support program for asylum seekers for almost ten years. Based in Sydney, he had been active in strengthening the capacity of the Uyghur communities in Australia and beyond. He is currently managing a project supporting the implementation of voice recognition of nationalities for the purposes of asylum seeker identification, implemented in Turkey.

He is the former president of the Australian Uyghur Association and continues to support his community and raise awareness of the issues facing Uyghurs through arranging international conferences. He has also published the following articles: "China's Use of Psychological Warfare against the Uyghurs" in *Foreign Policy* (2018); "Turn in the Two-Faced: the Plight of Uyghur Intellectuals" in *The Diplomat* (2018); "Xi Jinping's Genocide of the Uyghurs" in *Foreign Policy* (2018); and "Underneath the Trade War of Donald Trump and Xi Jinping" in *Foreign Policy* (2018).